MODERN
Scandinavian
BAKING

MODERN
Scandinavian
A Cookbook of Sweet
Treats and Savory Bakes
BAKING

DAYTONA STRONG

Creator of Outside Oslo

Photography by Marija Vidal

R

ROCKRIDGE
PRESS

For general information on our other products and services or to obtain technical support, please contact our Customer Care Department within the United States at (866) 744-2665, or outside the United States at (510) 253-0500.

Rockridge Press publishes its books in a variety of electronic and print formats. Some content that appears in print may not be available in electronic books, and vice versa.

Interior and Cover Designer: Patricia Fabricant
Art Producer: Michael Hardgrove
Editor: Rebecca Markley
Production Editor: Nora Milman

Photography © 2020 Marija Vidal. Food styling by Elisabet der Nederlanden
Author photo courtesy of © Rosemary Dai Ross

ISBN: Print 978-1-64611-618-8 | eBook 978-1-64611-619-5

R1

In memory of my grandmothers,
Agny Johanne Danielsen and
Adeline Ingeborg Midstokke,
for their humble generosity,
graceful hospitality, enduring legacy,
and unconditional love

Contents

Introduction

SCANDINAVIANS KNOW THE COLD. They've experienced the chill that hangs in the air, almost tangible, and how it seeps through the cells of the body. There's a reason they bundle up in those thick, iconic knit sweaters! I grew up in Seattle where the chill of winter is relatively mild, but still I know what it's like to stand out in the cold at my grandparents' door, waiting for them to welcome me in. I've experienced what it's like when that door opens and the heat from inside—accompanied by the aromas of Grandma's cooking—spills out. I know the taste of all her buttery cookies and the delight of biting into a delicate *krumkake* with my hand ready to catch the crumbs as it shatters between my teeth. Indeed, Scandinavian baking is tied to hospitality, and just as biting into a cinnamon bun still hot from the oven warms the body, baking helps facilitate relationships, which warms hearts.

Baking is an integral part of Scandinavian food culture, as much a part of the day as a cup of coffee might be here in the United States. Consider *fika*, for example—the Swedish coffee break. In this lovely tradition, stopping to connect with someone is inseparably linked to enjoying something buttery and baked and delicious. Cozy, right? That brings me to another Scandinavian concept—*hygge*—and its Norwegian counterpart, *kos* and *koselig*. While all those terms could simply translate to "cozy" (and you need a lot of that during the long, cold winters!), there's so much more to them: They reflect a mindset that is essential to the culture. And while you can't achieve real *hygge* by simply whipping up something sweet, the act of baking certainly helps get you closer to the essence of that lifestyle.

As a journalist and food writer, I've been studying the food of Scandinavia for over a decade, since I launched my blog, *Outside Oslo* (www.outside-oslo.com), in 2009. I write about Scandinavian food because I believe that one of the most profound ways we can show love and extend hospitality and acceptance to those around us is with food.

My family's roots burrow deep into Norwegian and Norwegian American history. With a dad who emigrated from Norway as a preteen and a mother who's also Norwegian, by way of North Dakota, baking was a significant part of our family culture. My childhood memories are studded with baked treats—delicate *krumkaker*, soft potato *lefse* rolled up with butter and sugar, tins of buttery cookies of countless shapes and variations, pillowy layer cakes draped with marzipan. The generations that came before me seemed to always be ready to serve something special for unexpected company—an essential part of the hospitality that they demonstrated so well.

I may live in Seattle, far outside of Oslo—the city of my father's birth—but I try to create my own little slice of Scandinavian hospitality and flavor right where I am through the meals I prepare and the beauty and atmosphere I create in my home. No matter what heritage and personal background you have, I hope this book will inspire you to do the same.

ONE

The Art and Heart of Scandinavian Baking

WHEN WE BAKE WITH LOVE, THAT'S WHEN BEAUTY COMES INTO OUR CREATIONS. That was my message at a baking class I taught in Seattle some years ago. I was teaching the art of Norwegian coffee treats, some of which take practice and finesse to get just right. But in my experience—as the granddaughter of a couple of women devoted to the art of hospitality—the quality of a cookie or pastry certainly matters, but not as much as the love it's prepared and served with. After all, when you bake from your heart, the sentiment works its way into each cup of flour measured, each component mixed into the dough, and each beautiful, finished confection. As you flag the recipes in this book that you'd like to try, keep in mind the loving intention behind Scandinavian baking. In this chapter, I'll equip you with foundations, techniques, and tools you'll need to extend this sort of delicious hospitality to the people in your life.

UNDERSTANDING THE CULTURE THROUGH FOOD

While you don't need an introduction to appreciate the deliciousness of a Roasted Strawberry Danish Braid (that recipe is on page 66 by the way), I want your enjoyment of the recipes to extend beyond that. When you understand the recipes' cultural and historical contexts, you'll come to appreciate them all the more.

For example, do you know how buttery baked goods became a symbol of selfless hospitality in Scandinavian culture? Way before Norway became one of the richest countries in the world after the discovery of oil in the 1960s, those in the less-well-off classes would sell their home-made butter most months of the year and only use it for themselves at Christmastime. Therefore, the wide variety of butter-based Norwegian cookies hint at the extravagance people showered upon their loved ones during that holiday. And that's just one slice of insight into the role food (and especially baking) plays in the cultures of Scandinavia.

NORWAY

For many years when it was under Danish and Swedish rule, Norway lacked the resources and means of its neighboring countries. It also has less than 3 percent arable land. Today, the economic climate in Norway is much different, and the culture has changed dramatically, but the geography remains the same. Many of the flavors I associate with Norway are so rooted in the seasons and the land that they aren't going anywhere. (Think fish from the frigid waters, berries ripened in the summer sun, mushrooms from verdant forests, and creamy butter fresh from the farm.) You'll see Norway represented in this book with recipes like my favorite rhubarb cake, a sculptural array of buttery cookies, and of course my own personal recipe for *gløgg* to accompany the Christmas recipes. Because, after all, Norwegians work hard—but they also know how to enjoy life to the fullest.

DENMARK

When it comes to food, Denmark is arguably the most refined of the Scandinavian countries. The country has a long history of royalty (its monarchy is one of the oldest in the world) and wealth. Plus, the country has been among the top 10 richest countries in the world at various points throughout the last several centuries. Denmark is home to a plethora of rich and delicious pastries. Take the *weinerbrød*, or Danish, for example—layers of yeasted laminated buttery dough filled with custard or berry preserves. That certainly wouldn't have been peasant food.

Beyond sweets, the country's baking legacy includes *rugbrød*—a hearty whole-meal bread that is dense and dark, full of nutrition, and boasts a toothsome texture. *Rugbrød* is typically used for *smørrebrød*, open-faced sandwiches that are most definitely knife-and-fork fare.

SWEDEN

If Denmark is known for *hygge* and Norway *koselig*, then Sweden offers the world *fika* and *lagom* (more on *hygge* and *fika* on pages 4 and 7). Many Americans will recognize the Swedish traditions people take part in on St. Lucia's Day—or at least the iconic image of a girl dressed in white and wearing a wreath of candles—and most can envision revelers dancing around a flower-clad pole on Midsummer. In addition to the saffron-scented buns and strawberry layer cakes that accompany Sweden's beloved holidays, some of this country's best baked goods, in my opinion, are Swedish pancakes, cinnamon rolls, marzipan-cloaked princess cake, and the fudgy chocolate *kladdkaka*.

SPECIAL INGREDIENTS

I have made a point of making the recipes in this book accessible to the home baker. Most of the ingredients and equipment should be easy to find at many grocery and home kitchen stores. There are, however, instances in which a special ingredient or tool might be required. For example, no Scandinavian baking book would be complete without the heart-shaped waffles on page 54. Plus, some ingredients—like lingonberries—help define the flavors of Scandinavian baking and are therefore worth tracking down (see Resources on page 124). Here's a look at some of the less-common ingredients I'd recommend for your Scandinavian baking pantry.

GRAINS AND FLOURS

Wheat Flour

At first glance, this seems basic—obvious, really. But is it? Perusing a well-stocked grocery aisle, one might encounter everything from the average white all-purpose flour to specialty grains like einkorn and spelt. For the purposes of this book, we'll mostly be using unbleached all-purpose flour, stone-ground whole-wheat flour, unbleached bread flour, and cake flour.

HYGGE!

As you bake your way through this book, your home will be filled with the aromas of cinnamon and cardamom, vanilla and cloves, and butter and yeast—cozy indeed. And that brings me to *hygge* (pronounced HOO-gah), the Danish term for a warm, cozy lifestyle and an emphasis on well-being. The essence of *hygge* is embraced throughout Scandinavia, but it can be complex to explain, because it's about more than just cozy things. It's an approach to life that involves slowing down and spending quality time with others. (Norway has a similar word, *kos* or *koselig*.)

That said, the kitchen seems like a natural place to concoct such evocative and comforting feelings. After all, food is a way to nurture and nourish our loved ones with hospitality and open hearts.

I personally embrace *hygge* by spending as much heartfelt time as possible with my family. I invite my children into the kitchen to watch butter and sugar transform into any number of sweet treats, much like spinning gold. Each night I serve them dinner, it brings me comfort to know I've selected healthy ingredients and prepared the meal with love. *Hygge*, to me, is about balance—about the memories, the small things, that will hopefully stay with us because they're connected to a feeling of love.

As a mother, I take pleasure in baking with my children, knowing that each time I fill the kitchen with the scent of cardamom and other warm spices, I'm creating the backdrop for memories that will linger with them for the rest of their lives, just like the memories that I collected in my youth.

Rye Flour

This whole-grain flour is common in Scandinavian baking and an essential ingredient in the Danish *rugbrød* and many other breads. The gluten-forming protein in rye is lower than wheat, resulting in a longer leavening period and a denser loaf.

Barley

Barley is the oldest grain in the Nordic region. Due to its low gluten content, it won't produce fluffy bread on its own but can be great for flatbreads. I won't be using barley flour in this book, but barley flakes appear in the Grains of the North Buns (*rundstykker*) on page 24.

Oats

Oats figure prominently in a number of Scandinavian recipes, from breads and porridges to cookies and balls, such as my grandmother's *bryte havrekaker*—"broken" oatmeal cookies—on page 107, and the Danish no-bake *chokladbollar* on page 119. They naturally contain no gluten. However, if you're avoiding gluten, be sure to check the label to find a designated gluten-free product, as it's often processed with the same equipment as other grains.

SPICES

Cardamom

Cardamom, with its pungent perfume reminiscent of sandalwood and a grandfather's cologne, is one of the quintessential spices of Scandinavian baking. Its scent—earthy and exotic—is commonly used to flavor *krumkaker*, *vafler*, and a variety of other traditional treats and cakes. Do yourself a favor and grind your own (see information about spice grinders on the page 8)—the results are incomparable. I keep cardamom seeds in a simple manual spice grinder dedicated to this ingredient.

Saffron

Saffron is widely regarded as one of the most expensive spices in the world. That said, a little goes a long way, and you won't be using it often when baking Scandinavian treats. Perhaps most notably, it appears in the *lussekatter* or St. Lucia Buns (page 50) to be served on St. Lucia's Day in December.

Caraway

An essential flavor in the world of Scandinavian cooking and baking, caraway can be found in many rye-based breads and crackers, such as *knekkebrød* (page 28) and *sirupslimpa* (page 22).

LEAVENING AGENTS

Yeast

The recipes in this book make use of active dry yeast, rather than fresh or instant, for the sake of accessibility and consistency. If you opt to buy a jar instead of packets, store it in the freezer after opening it to extend its shelf life. A helpful note: There are 2¼ teaspoons in one packet of active dry yeast.

Baking Soda and Baking Powder

These two chemical leaveners will aerate your yeast-free baked goods and give them a pleasant crumb. Baking soda is sodium bicarbonate, which requires a liquid and an acid for its reaction to happen. Baking powder consists of the same chemical compound, with the addition of a powdered acid. The use of these two leaveners differs—for example, the kind of reactions they produce and how they balance the acidity, which impacts flavor. Feel free to read up more on these if you're interested—it's actually pretty interesting baking science.

Baker's Ammonia (aka Ammonium Carbonate, Salt of Hartshorn, Hornsalt)

An ingredient made from ground antlers? Yep, although these days it's made differently. Use it to make the meltingly crisp (contradiction?) Swedish vanilla "dream" cookies on page 100. Be warned, it lets off a strong odor while baking, but the aroma dissipates quickly and the crisp results are well worth the brief stench. Store it in the freezer if you'll be keeping it for a long time. If you can't find baker's ammonia, substitute with equal parts baking powder and baking soda.

OTHER INGREDIENTS

Berries (Fresh and as Preserves)

Berries of all varieties are important in Scandinavia, and there are two in particular that evoke the North: lingonberries and cloudberries. Look for them in the form of preserves at well-stocked grocery stores and shops. Cloudberries form the foundation of *multekrem* (used as a filling for the

SHALL WE FIKA?

Fragrant with the warm aromas of cinnamon, freshly ground cardamom, and hot, buttery yeasted dough, a Scandinavian cinnamon-cardamom bun is the perfect accompaniment for a cup of coffee. Add a true pause and intention to savor the moment and connect with someone, and you have *fika*.

The word *fika* comes from an old Swedish word for coffee—*kaffi*. Simply invert the syllables and you get *fika*. Essentially, *fika* is a coffee break. But it isn't just any coffee break. In Scandinavian culture, coffee isn't just something ordered from a drive-through window or consumed at a table in a coffee shop surrounded by silent strangers. Coffee accompanies conversation. It goes hand-in-hand with friendship, with conviviality, with time spent leisurely with someone. Notice the similarities between *fika* and *hygge* (page 4)?

While coziness can manifest itself in a lot of different ways, from plush blankets and flickering candlelight to thick sweaters and scarves, we'd do well to consider community an integral part of it.

krumkaker on page 114). They're on the pricy side but are worth it for a special occasion. Use some for *multekrem*, then savor any remainders later on one of the homemade breads in chapter 2.

Sugars

Stock up on granulated sugar, as you'll need it for nearly all the recipes in this book! While you're at it, make sure you have confectioners' sugar on hand, and try to track down Swedish pearl sugar for the distinctive topping on buns like Cinnamon and Cardamom Twists (page 46). I also occasionally call for *vaniljesukker*, or Scandinavian vanilla sugar. You can find it online and at Scandinavian stores and gourmet markets. Otherwise, it's incredibly easy to make: Although Scandinavian *vaniljesukker* is made with synthetic vanillin instead of real vanilla, you can mimic its flavor by simply infusing confectioners' sugar—rather than granulated sugar—with a vanilla bean. Or feel free to mix a little vanilla extract into confectioners' sugar in a pinch.

Syrups

Golden syrup is a great alternative to the light and dark syrups of Scandinavia, and it can be found in the baking aisles of many well-stocked grocery stores. Use golden syrup in *sirupslimpa* (page 22), *pepperkaker* (page 112), *bondkakor* (page 104), and *havreflarn* (page 118). Honey and molasses can often be used instead, but they will yield different results.

Almonds (and All Manner of Almond Products)

Almonds are an essential part of Scandinavian baking: You can find them in many forms, including almond flour, sliced almonds, almond paste, and marzipan. I make use of all forms of almonds frequently, occasionally accenting them with a touch of almond extract.

EQUIPMENT

Here's a look at the basic tools you'll need to make the recipes in this book, and the specialty items you may wish to purchase if you don't own them already. (Turn to the Resources section on page 124 for a list of stores and online shops where you can find Scandinavian baking equipment.)

BREAD AND CAKE PANS

Most of the cakes in this book call for an 8-inch or 9-inch springform pan. Feel free to use either an 8½-by-4½-inch or a 9-by-5-inch loaf pan for the breads and the tiger cake (page 84). You'll want a 13-by-4-by-4-inch Pullman pan (also called a *pain de mie* pan) to give the Danish rye bread (*rugbrød*) its characteristic shape.

DIGITAL INSTANT-READ THERMOMETER

If you don't already have one of these in your kitchen, it's a useful tool for everything from checking the internal temperature of bread to making sure meats are cooked through.

SPICE GRINDER

Freshly ground spices can make a world of difference in baked goods. Once I tried it with cardamom, I never looked back. While I keep a manual grinder solely devoted to cardamom, feel free to get one to use for other spices as well—even a simple coffee grinder will work. It's a fantastic tool that deserves a place in every kitchen.

CAST IRON PANS

I love using my cast iron pans for *pannekaker* (page 56). Clean and season them properly (no soap or scouring!) and they will last a lifetime. Some people like to hunt for cast iron pans at secondhand or thrift stores (that's how durable they are!), though it's easy to find new ones for reasonable prices at kitchen stores and online.

ROLLING PIN

Useful for cookies, flatbreads, tarts, and pies. Choose one you like the shape and length of, whether it's a roller with handles or a tapered French rolling pin. Also, consider getting a corrugated pin for *lefse* (page 26) or a notched one for other flatbreads.

LEFSE SUPPLIES

Speaking of *lefse*, if you're planning on making this Norwegian flatbread from time to time, consider buying these tools and pieces of equipment: potato ricer, griddle, cloth-covered pastry board, corrugated rolling pin with cloth cover, turning stick, and pastry brush. Otherwise, simply use a large skillet, regular rolling pin, and other tools you have on hand.

BAKING TECHNIQUES

I've written the recipes in this book in such a way that they should explain the processes for themselves. However, it's always helpful to keep some basics in mind.

LEAVENING AND PROOFING

The "magic" of watching yeast work never gets old. Somehow, this micro-organism that's been used since ancient times fills me with wonder even today, as I watch it begin to proof and then work its magic in a loaf of bread. That said, working with yeast used to intimidate me until I learned the basics. For the recipes in this book, which use active dry yeast, proof the yeast in a little water or milk that's 110°F until the mixture foams. To let the dough rise, find a warm place that's free of drafts.

BAKER'S DOZEN

Follow these 13 rules to achieve the best results with the recipes in this book—or any other baking recipes, for that matter. An organized, efficient, and mindful approach—plus lots of love—will yield the most delicious, perfectly textured baked goods every time.

READ THE RECIPE FIRST!

I almost hate to mention it, but I know that I need the reminder sometimes, too. By reading the recipe before you begin, you ensure that you have all the ingredients on hand and won't encounter any surprises (like a prep-in-advance step) in the middle of the baking process.

START WITH MISE EN PLACE

Employ this practice—which essentially translates to "everything in its place"—by gathering all your tools and preparing and measuring all your ingredients in advance. You'll set yourself up for success as you progress through the steps of the recipe.

KNOW YOUR OVEN

So 350°F is 350°F, right? Technically, yes. But that doesn't mean your oven is necessarily calibrated to heat precisely to that temperature, or that the temperature will be consistent throughout your oven. Buy a simple oven thermometer (I bought mine for only $7) and make adjustments as needed. Also, make sure you preheat your oven thoroughly, giving it ample time to heat up, and take note of hot spots in your oven and rotate pans as needed so your creations bake evenly.

MEASURE INGREDIENTS PROPERLY

To measure flour without a scale, loosen it up with a spoon first if it's packed tightly. Then, spoon the flour into the measuring cup and level it off with the flat side of a knife. For brown sugar, which can also differ in weight depending on how it's measured, fill the measuring cup or spoon and use the spoon or your fingers to press it down tightly into the cup. You don't need to worry about this with granulated sugar.

USE HIGH-QUALITY INGREDIENTS

Seriously. Bad butter makes for a bad batter.

INGREDIENT TEMPERATURE MATTERS

Don't cut corners if a recipe calls for room temperature butter or eggs and yours are still chilled. The same goes with letting melted butter cool to lukewarm if instructed. When I know I'll be baking a recipe that calls for room temperature butter—such as the heart-shaped waffles on page 54—I set the butter on the counter the night before or first thing in the morning so it will be ready when I need it.

On the other hand, make sure heated ingredients aren't too warm—you don't want to kill yeast, for example, with liquid that's too warm or butter that's still hot from melting.

ADD INGREDIENTS IN THE ORDER LISTED

The order of ingredients and recipe steps are very intentional in baking; altering the sequence of these recipe components can result in a much different outcome than you intended.

DON'T WASTE A MOMENT

When baking cakes, keep moving. After you mix the batter, bake the cake immediately so that the leavening doesn't weaken.

FIND THE RIGHT SPOT FOR BAKING

Always place your bake in the middle of the center rack of the oven unless the recipe says otherwise. This will allow for the best air circulation and even baking.

DON'T LET IT BROWN TOO FAST

It's not uncommon for a bread, cake, or pastry to darken too quickly when the interior is still underbaked. If you notice that your baked good is browning midway through baking, simply shield the top of your creation with a sheet of foil for the remainder of the baking time.

COOL YOUR BREADS PROPERLY

As tempting as it is to slice into a loaf of bread still hot from the oven, many loaves will continue to bake as they cool, so if you cut into it prematurely you risk encountering an underdone crumb. It's generally okay for the bread to still be warm, but do give it a chance to amply rest.

USE A COOLING RACK

Transfer cookies to a wire rack as soon as they come out of the oven so they won't continue to bake too much on the baking sheet. If you've used parchment paper to line the baking sheet, simply slide the whole thing off.

GIVE IT YOUR HEART

The beautiful thing about baking cookies, cakes, and pastries is that they are not objects of necessity, but rather expressions of love. Give yourself plenty of time and eliminate distractions—put your heart into it, and enjoy sharing your love with those you treasure most.

KNEADING DOUGH

Kneading and rising, or proofing, are two key tasks that work together to create an excellent loaf of bread. Kneading dough develops the gluten, an important step in achieving a glorious chew. While many people choose to do this in a stand mixer, I know that not every kitchen will have one of these, plus I love the almost-meditative process of working the dough by hand. In general, expect to knead yeasted doughs for about 10 minutes by hand (unless the recipe states otherwise). Be sure to avoid adding too much flour on your kneading surface.

KNOWING WHEN YOUR BAKE IS DONE

Bread

Take the guesswork out of determining when your bread is done with a couple of simple tips: Give it a tap on the bottom and listen for a hollow sound. Take it a step further with an instant-read digital thermometer—my preferred method for its specificity! Many breads are done at 190°F; if it's enriched with butter, milk, or eggs, it may need to be 200°F. Either way, give these methods a try to ensure that your creation is baked to perfection.

Cake

To start, use the toothpick test: A toothpick inserted in the center should come out clean. Also look for these cues: The edges have begun to pull away from the pan, the top should be golden brown (in the case of light cakes), and the top should spring back when you press a finger on it. Look for an internal temperature of 190° to 205°F, depending on the cake.

Cookies

The cues will vary based on the type of cookie, but here are a few general rules. Are the edges firm but the middle is just set? They might be done. Always err on the side of caution and check cookies on the early side—and keep in mind that they will keep baking a little after you take them out of the oven. Ultimately, be sure to read the recipe and pay attention to its visual cues.

Pastry

Whether you're working with puff pastry or Danish pastry dough, a look at that honey-brown flaky crust will tell you a lot about what you need to know. Is it richly golden brown? Has it puffed up? You should be good to go.

ABOUT THE RECIPES

Okay, now we come to the exciting part: the recipes! In the chapters that follow, you'll find tried-and-true recipes that bakers of all levels can enjoy making. Some came from my grandmother, and I am so grateful that I was able to learn from her in a hands-on setting rather than merely reading a recipe. With that in mind, I have made it a point to write the recipes—especially those that require special techniques (such as *lefse*, *krumkaker*, and *sandkaker*)—in such a way that guides you through the process and anticipates where you might have questions. To help you understand the diversity within Scandinavian baking, each recipe features the flag of its country of origin. And for easy reference (because Scandinavia is especially known for its Christmas confections), I've compiled winter holiday recipes in a special list at the end of the book.

A note about food restrictions and special diets: I believe that the essence of the Norwegian hospitality my grandparents shared includes a sensitivity to those with food restrictions based on health needs and personal convictions. While this book is not diet-focused, it does help you cater to the needs of your guests—and yourself—with labels signaling which recipes comply with several major restrictions, including gluten-free, dairy-free, nut-free, egg-free, and vegetarian or vegan. You'll also find variations that adjust for allergens and sensitivities when possible.

Let's get started!

COUNTRY FLAGS

NORWAY

SWEDEN

DENMARK

Breads and Other Savory Bakes

IN HER LATER YEARS, GRANDMA ADELINE'S HANDS revealed her age. Skin like vellum covered her swollen knuckles, and heavy gold rings spun loosely on thinning fingers. But when she would make potato *lefse*—a traditional Norwegian flatbread—those same hands were anything but frail.

As Grandma worked flour into a bowl of riced potatoes, her strength and muscle memory far outshone her weak bones and aging body. She had been a professional *lefse* baker, after all.

I learned to bake *lefse* and some of the other Scandinavian recipes in this book from her. As we baked, I'd ask questions, trying to coax out her history. Grandma wasn't great with details, but I cherished the stories that would emerge as her hands moved, as though resuming those old baking techniques released something in her aging mind.

Lefse is woven into the fabric of my life as a Norwegian American. However, as you'll soon discover, it's only a slice (pun intended) of Scandinavian bread culture.

Whole-grain breads are a staple of the Scandinavian diet, and a hearty whole-wheat loaf named after the naturopath and priest Sebastian Kneipp is said to be the most popular bread in Norway. Use this bread, based on that classic, for anything from sandwiches to toast smeared with butter and your favorite jam.

Hearty No-Knead Whole-Wheat Bread

KNEIPPBRØD

DAIRY-FREE, NUT-FREE, EGG-FREE, VEGETARIAN

MAKES: 1 loaf

PREP TIME: 20 minutes, plus 2½ hours to rise

COOK TIME: 40 minutes

1 teaspoon active dry yeast

2 cups warm water (110°F), divided

¼ teaspoon sugar

2 tablespoons honey

1 tablespoon canola oil

3 cups stone-ground whole-wheat flour

½ cup bulgur

3 tablespoons vital wheat gluten

2 teaspoons salt

1. In a large mixing bowl, dissolve the yeast in ½ cup of the warm water with the sugar; give it about 10 minutes to proof. Stir in the remaining water, honey, and oil. Add the flour, bulgur, vital wheat gluten, and salt, stirring with a wooden spoon to combine—you should immediately see the strands of gluten develop. Cover with a clean tea towel. Let rise until doubled, about 2 hours.

2. Lightly grease a loaf pan (8½-by-4½-inch or 9-by-5-inch should work). Transfer the dough to the pan and let rise for another 30 minutes or so.

3. Meanwhile, preheat the oven to 400°F. Bake for about 40 minutes, covering with foil midway if it darkens prematurely, until the top is a deep golden brown and the bread reaches an internal temperature of 190°F. It should make a hollow sound when you remove it from the pan and tap the bottom.

4. Remove from pan and transfer to a wire rack to cool completely before slicing.

VARIATION TIP: Make this recipe vegan by using molasses instead of honey.

STORAGE TIP: Like so many homemade breads, this loaf is best the day it's made. However, you can store any leftovers in a covered container at room temperature for up to 2 days.

I have a thing for old church cookbooks. I'd like to think that the parishioners submitted only recipes they were particularly proud of. Some years ago I combed through an old cookbook from the Seattle church where a number of my relatives worshipped back in the day. In it I found a trove of old family recipes, including Grandma Adeline's oatmeal bread. While I don't know its origins before it made it to her, I do know that loaves like this exist in Scandinavia, too. I've adapted the recipe to my taste, and I hope you love it as much as I do.

Grandma Adeline's Honey-Kissed Oatmeal Bread
HAVREBRØD/GRÖTBRÖD

NUT-FREE, EGG-FREE, VEGETARIAN

MAKES: 2 loaves
PREP TIME: 30 minutes, plus 1 hour 10 minutes to rise
COOK TIME: 45 minutes

2 cups cold water

1 cup old-fashioned rolled oats, plus 2 tablespoons, for topping

¼ cup honey

¼ cup sugar, divided

3 tablespoons butter

1 packet (2¼ teaspoons) active dry yeast

½ cup lukewarm water (110°F)

3 cups unbleached bread flour

1 cup stone-ground whole-wheat flour

2 teaspoons salt

1. To prepare the oatmeal, bring the cold water to a boil in a small pot. Stir in the oats and reduce to a simmer, stirring occasionally for 5 minutes. Remove from heat and stir in the honey, most of the sugar (reserving ½ teaspoon or so for the yeast), and the butter; stir until the butter is melted. Let cool until lukewarm.

2. In a large mixing bowl, dissolve the yeast in the lukewarm water with the reserved sugar, and allow it to sit until it bubbles, 5 to 10 minutes.

3. Add the oatmeal, bread flour, whole-wheat flour, and salt and stir to combine. (Add an additional ½ cup bread flour if necessary to bring the dough together.) Turn out the dough onto a lightly floured surface and knead for about 5 minutes, or until the dough comes together and releases some of its stickiness (a bench scraper will help separate the dough from the surface as you work).

4. Transfer the dough to an oiled bowl, cover with a clean tea towel, and let rise at room temperature for about 40 minutes—it won't quite double but should have some good lift.

5. Lightly grease 2 loaf pans (8½-by-4½-inch or 9-by-5-inch should work). Shape the dough into 2 loaves and fit them into the pans. Let them rise, covered with a clean tea towel, for an additional 30 minutes.

6. Meanwhile, preheat the oven to 350°F.

7. Score the tops of the loaves a few times each with a sharp knife. Top the loaves with the remaining 2 tablespoons of oats. Bake for about 35 minutes, or until the loaves are golden brown, sound hollow if you remove them from the pans and give them a thump, or reach an internal temperature of about 200°F. Remove the loaves from the pans and let them cool completely on a wire rack before slicing and serving.

SERVING TIP: Elevate any bread with homemade butter! Vigorously shake 1 cup of heavy whipping cream and ½ teaspoon of salt in a screw-top jar until the cream separates into solid and liquid parts. Be patient—it takes up to 30 minutes to turn from whipped cream to butter. Strain and discard the liquid.

VARIATION: Simply swap in a vegan butter alternative for the butter to make this bread dairy-free, and swap in molasses for the honey to make it vegan.

An essential recipe in a Scandinavian baker's repertoire, this loaf is the basis of the *smørrebrød* (*smørbrød* in Norwegian), the quintessential Scandinavian open sandwich. Do yourself a favor and track down the rye chops (essentially cracked rye berries) and the 13-inch Pullman pan (see tip) that gives this loaf its characteristic shape. The slightly tart and toothsome, dense loaf is nutritious, low in fat, and full of flavor—proving how delicious doing your body good can be. Please take note that you'll need to begin the process a day or two in advance.

Classic Rye Bread
■■ RUGBRØD

NUT-FREE, EGG-FREE, VEGETARIAN

MAKES: 1 loaf

PREP TIME: 30 minutes, plus overnight to soak and 4 to 5 hours to rise

COOK TIME: 1 hour 10 minutes

2½ cups rye chops (aka cracked rye berries; find them online or at specialty stores)

1 cup seeds (¼ cup each sunflower, flax, sesame, and pumpkin)

2 cups boiling water, divided

3 cups dark rye flour

1¼ teaspoons active dry yeast

½ cup lukewarm water (110°F)

¼ teaspoon sugar

1 cup unbleached bread flour

1 cup buttermilk

2 tablespoons molasses

2 tablespoons salt

DAY 1:

In a medium bowl, stir together the rye chops and sunflower, flax, sesame, and pumpkin seeds. Pour 1 cup of boiling water over the top and stir to combine. In another medium bowl, stir 1 cup of boiling water into the rye flour. Cover each bowl loosely with a clean tea towel and let them sit overnight at room temperature.

DAY 2:

1. In a small bowl, dissolve the yeast in the lukewarm water with the sugar and let sit until it bubbles, 5 to 10 minutes.

2. In a large mixing bowl, combine the yeast, soaked rye and seeds, soaked rye flour, bread flour, buttermilk, molasses, and salt. Stir well, then work with your hands until all the flour and seeds are incorporated.

3. Let rise, covered with a clean tea towel, for 2 hours. Spray a Pullman loaf pan with baking spray. Place the dough in the pan and let it rise until it reaches within an inch of the top of the pan, another 2 to 3 hours.

4. Preheat the oven to 400°F. Bake for 1 hour and 10 minutes, or until the bread reaches an internal temperature of 210°F. (Cover it with foil midway through baking to prevent it from darkening too quickly.)

OPEN-FACED SANDWICHES WITH SMOKED SALMON, ARUGULA, AND DILL
RØGET LAKS SMØRREBRØD MED ARUGULA OG DILL

NUT-FREE, EGG-FREE

MAKES: 2 servings
PREP TIME: 5 minutes

2 slices Classic Rye
  Bread (page 20)

2 tablespoons sour cream

2 tablespoons freshly
  grated horseradish

Pinch salt, up to
  ¼ teaspoon, to taste

2 ounces sliced
  smoked salmon

1 cup baby arugula

Dill wisps, for garnish

1. Place a slice of bread on each of two plates.

2. In a small bowl, combine the sour cream and horse-radish. Season with a pinch of salt, starting sparingly and keeping in mind that the saltiness of the salmon will impact the finished *smørrebrød*.

3. Spread the cream on each slice of bread, all the way to the edges. Arrange salmon slices evenly across the surface. Top with the arugula and garnish with fresh dill.

DID YOU KNOW? *Smørrebrød* are one of those things that defy borders in Scandinavia. The Danes may be particularly known for these delightful open-faced sandwiches, but Norwegians and Swedes love them just as much. Having grown up with *smørrebrød*—or *smørbrød* as it's spelled in Norwegian—I'll take one of these over a two-slice American sandwich any day. *Smørrebrød* are loaded with protein-rich ingredients and are basically a complete meal and a work of art on a slice of bread. What's not to love?

5. Set the pan on a wire rack and let the bread cool completely before removing—this will take several hours. Then, ideally, give it another day to fully set before slicing into it.

STORAGE TIP: This is the rare loaf of bread that gets better with time. It will peak after a day or two and stay fresh for at least several days. Store it, covered in paper, at room temperature, or freeze.

TIP: A specialty pan truly makes a difference for this bread. You want the loaf and its slices to have that characteristic squarish shape. I bought my 13-by-4-by-4-inch Pullman loaf pan—also called a *pain de mie* pan—from King Arthur Flour's website (see Resources).

Get ready for the most fragrant baking experience. This slightly sweet rye dough is scented with fennel, anise, and caraway seeds, along with orange zest. It's often served at Christmastime, but is a treat any time you're in the mood for something cozy.

Rye and Syrup Bread with Fennel, Anise, Caraway, and Orange

SIRUPSLIMPA

NUT-FREE, EGG-FREE, VEGETARIAN

MAKES: 1 loaf
PREP TIME: 35 minutes, plus 2½ hours to rise
COOK TIME: 1 hour

4 tablespoons butter

2 cups milk

1 packet (2¼ teaspoons) active dry yeast

½ teaspoon sugar

½ cup golden syrup, plus more for brushing

Grated zest of 1 organic orange, about 3 tablespoons

1 tablespoon salt

1 teaspoon each fennel, anise, and caraway seeds, crushed (see Technique Tip)

3¼ cups unbleached bread flour

2¼ cups rye flour

1. In a small pan, melt the butter. Add the milk and heat it to 110°F, using a digital thermometer. Pour a little of the hot butter and milk mixture over the yeast and sugar in a mixing bowl and proof until it bubbles, 5 to 10 minutes. Then stir the remaining butter and milk mixture into the yeast mixture, along with the syrup, orange zest, salt, fennel, anise, and caraway seeds.

2. Add the bread flour and rye flour and stir to combine, then turn the dough out onto a lightly floured surface and knead for 10 minutes, adding a little more bread flour if needed. The dough will be quite sticky, but it should still be workable with the help of a bench scraper. Transfer the dough to a lightly greased bowl, cover with a clean tea towel, and let rise until doubled, about 1½ hours.

3. Punch down the dough and knead for a minute, then shape it into a round loaf. Transfer to a baking sheet lined with parchment paper and let rise again, covered with a clean tea towel, until almost doubled, about 1 hour.

4. Preheat the oven to 375°F. Prick the top of the dough all over with a toothpick or skewer. Bake until it reaches an internal temperature of 190°F, about 1 hour. (Cover with foil if it darkens too quickly.)

5. Remove the bread from the oven and transfer it to a wire rack. Brush the top with more syrup mixed with a little water. Let cool completely before serving.

TECHNIQUE TIP: Pulse the fennel, anise, and caraway seeds in a coffee grinder a few times to crush them, or simply use a mortar and pestle.

VARIATION TIP: Golden syrup is worth tracking down for this recipe, as well as for the *pepperkaker* on page 112. If you can't find it, feel free to use molasses instead, although it will yield a subtly different flavor.

Wheat, rye, barley, and oats are important elements of Scandinavian baking, and these hearty buns contain them all. *Rundstykker*—which translates to round pieces—are known throughout Scandinavia in various forms. Some of the most common are simply wheat buns with poppy seeds on top, but they are open to interpretation. I've chosen to make mine with the four grains that are representative of the North. If you can't get ahold of barley flakes, feel free to improvise and replace their quantity with oats. As an extra-special treat, cut these buns in half while still warm and spread them with butter. Or serve with cheese or jam, and (of course) a cup of coffee.

Grains of the North Buns

RUNDSTYKKER

NUT-FREE, VEGETARIAN

MAKES: 8 buns
PREP TIME: 35 minutes, plus 2½ hours to rise
COOK TIME: 12 minutes

½ cup old-fashioned rolled oats

½ cup barley flakes

3 tablespoons butter

1½ cups lukewarm milk (110°F)

1 packet (2¼ teaspoons) active dry yeast

1 teaspoon sugar

2 cups unbleached bread flour

1 cup dark rye flour

1½ teaspoons salt

Beaten egg, for glaze

Oat or barley flakes, for topping

Flaky salt, for topping

1. Pulse the oats and barley flakes in a food processor until finely ground.

2. In a small saucepan, melt the butter then add the milk, heating until the mixture reaches 110°F.

3. In a small bowl, combine the yeast and sugar. Pour in ½ cup of the butter and milk mixture and let the yeast proof for 5 to 10 minutes, or until it bubbles.

4. Pour the activated yeast into a large mixing bowl with the remaining milk, the oats and barley, bread flour, rye flour, and salt and stir to combine.

5. Turn out the dough onto a lightly floured surface and knead for about 10 minutes. Transfer to a lightly oiled bowl and let rise, covered with a clean tea towel, for about 2 hours, or until almost doubled.

6. Divide the dough into 8 equal pieces and shape each piece into a bun. Cover and let rise again for 30 minutes.

7. Meanwhile, preheat the oven to 425°F.

8. Brush the top of each bun with the beaten egg and sprinkle with oat or barley flakes and a touch of flaky salt. Bake for 10 to 12 minutes, or until the tops are golden and they make a hollow sound when you tap the bottom.

STORAGE TIP: While these are best the day they're made, you can also freeze them. Just thaw and then reheat in the oven.

SERVING TIP: Give these a try with homemade butter (see the Serving Tip on page 19) and a good sprinkling of flaky salt. Or, if you can get your hands on cloudberry preserves and Jarlsberg or Havarti cheese (from Norway and Denmark, respectively), the combination is divine.

Grandma Adeline was a professional *lefse* baker back in the day, and she made sure that Mom and I learned to make this soft potato flatbread properly. Whenever I see *lefse* recipes in cookbooks, I feel slightly bad for the reader who attempts to make it without a Norwegian grandma by their side, as it's very rooted in technique and practice. In this recipe, I've attempted to provide the next best thing with detailed instructions, and I'm delighted to share the tradition with you. Note that you will need to start this recipe the day before you plan to bake.

Grandma Adeline's Potato Lefse

POTETLEFSE

NUT-FREE, EGG-FREE, VEGETARIAN

MAKES: About 60 flatbreads
PREP TIME: 1 hour
COOK TIME: 2 hours

10 pounds russet potatoes

12 tablespoons (1½ sticks) butter, plus more at room temperature, for serving

¾ cup heavy cream

4½ tablespoons sugar

1 tablespoon salt

4½ cups all-purpose flour, plus more for rolling the dough

Sugar, for serving

Cinnamon, for serving

DAY 1:

1. Rinse and peel the potatoes, then place them in a large pot of boiling, salted water until cooked through—you want them to be thoroughly tender but not overcooked. Remove the potatoes from the heat and drain well.

2. When the potatoes are cool enough to touch, press them through a ricer, then measure 12 packed cups into a large bowl. Reserve the rest for another use.

3. In a medium saucepan, melt the butter. Stir in the cream, sugar, and salt. Pour the butter over the potatoes and stir to incorporate. When the mixture has cooled, cover and refrigerate it overnight.

DAY 2:

1. An hour or so before you're ready to get started, remove the potatoes from the refrigerator and let them come to room temperature.

2. Mix in the flour, using your hands to work all the ingredients together and massage out any lumps.

3. Shape the dough into balls about 2 inches in diameter and flatten them into disks, making sure they're solid and smooth without cracks. Place them on cookie sheets lined with waxed paper, and keep them in the refrigerator while you work—you want the dough to stay cool, so only remove about six disks at a time.

4. Set up your *lefse* rolling station and preheat a griddle or two large skillets. You'll need a surface on which to roll the *lefse*—I'd recommend a flour-covered pastry board, a rolling pin (ideally a cloth-covered corrugated one), a thin spatula or a turning stick, and a brush for removing excess flour. Sprinkle flour liberally over the board and rolling pin and rub it in to prevent the dough from sticking. (You'll repeat this when you're finished rolling each piece of dough—keeping a bowl full of flour at your workspace is helpful.)

5. Dip both sides of a dough disk into the flour, then place it on the board. Roll the *lefse*, using a medium touch, going in different directions to make a thin circle.

6. Gently slide a *lefse* stick or spatula under the *lefse*, a couple of inches from the edge. Carefully roll it over the stick to remove it from the board and transfer it to the hot griddle. (It's important to not let the *lefse* sit on the board long after rolling it, or it will stick.) When bubbles start to form on the surface of the *lefse*, lift up a corner to see if it is ready. There should be some brown spots on the underside. Flip and cook the other side.

7. Transfer the *lefse* to wax paper, and brush the flour off the finished *lefse* and the griddle. Cover the finished flatbreads with a clean tea towel while working to keep them soft. Flour the board and the rolling pin, and repeat with the remaining dough disks.

8. To serve, spread a warm *lefse* with butter and dust with sugar and cinnamon. Roll it up and cut it crosswise into 1½-inch-long pieces, or fold it into sixths.

STORAGE TIP: Fold each *lefse* into quarters and separate with a piece of wax paper. Wrap with wax paper or foil, then transfer to plastic bags, pressing out any air. These will stay fresh in the refrigerator for a few days and also freeze well.

VARIATION TIP: Folded or rolled, sweet or savory, there's no shortage of ways to enjoy *lefse*. One of the most common serving methods is to simply add butter and sugar and maybe a dusting of cinnamon before rolling it up. Feel free to use white or brown sugar—they're delicious both ways.

Flatbreads and crispbreads are important elements of Scandinavian food culture, and the Norwegian variety is one of my favorites. You can personalize *knekkebrød* by varying the seeds and grain to your liking. This *knekkebrød* is a wonderful backdrop to both sweet and savory toppings. I enjoy it with a cumin- and clove-spiced Norwegian cheese known as *nøkkelost* (or try Havarti with caraway if you can't find it), and also with high-quality and not-too-sweet cherry preserves.

Seeded Crispbread with Cherry Preserves and Cheese

▓▓ KNEKKEBRØD

DAIRY-FREE, NUT-FREE, EGG-FREE, VEGAN

MAKES: About 2 dozen crispbreads
PREP TIME: 15 minutes
COOK TIME: 20 minutes

1¼ cups old-fashioned rolled oats

⅓ cup dark rye flour

⅓ cup water

2 tablespoons olive oil

1 tablespoon maple syrup

¼ cup pumpkin seeds

¼ cup flax seeds

¼ cup raw sunflower seeds

¼ cup raw sesame seeds

1½ teaspoons salt

½ teaspoon caraway seeds

Flaky sea salt, for serving

Cheese, for serving (see headnote)

Tart cherry preserves, for serving

1. Preheat the oven to 350°F.

2. In a food processor, whirl the oats, rye flour, water, olive oil, and maple syrup together until a dough comes together and forms a ball. Transfer to a mixing bowl and add the pumpkin, flax, raw hulled sunflower, and raw, hulled sesame seeds, salt, and caraway and mix until combined.

3. Transfer the dough to a sheet of parchment paper and flatten it out as much as possible with your hands, aiming for a rough rectangle. Then top with another sheet of parchment paper and roll the dough with a rolling pin until it's as thin as possible—roughly ⅛ inch thick. Remove the top layer of parchment paper and slide the dough onto a large baking sheet. Sprinkle with flaky sea salt. Score into evenly sized rectangles. (Sizing is a matter of personal preference, but I find 2-by-3-inch rectangles to be a generally workable size.)

CONTINUED

4. Slide the baking sheet into the oven and bake for 10 minutes. Remove from the oven and very carefully flip the crispbread. Spritz with a little water and sprinkle with a little more sea salt. Return the baking sheet to the oven and continue to bake for another 10 minutes, or until the crispbread is crisp and golden. Allow the *knekkebrød* to cool on the baking sheet for about 5 minutes, or until it's easy to handle, then break it into rectangles and let them cool completely on wire racks.

5. Serve with cheese and cherry preserves.

STORAGE TIP: Stored in an airtight container, these should keep for about 2 weeks.

Like the Italian biscotti, *skorpor* are twice-baked buns or biscuits. They can be sweet or savory, and they're quite nice dunked into a cup of something hot. While the sweet varieties would be perfect with your afternoon coffee or tea, these savory little bites almost beg for a bowl of hot brothy soup, or eat them with a smear of butter and your favorite cheese.

Savory Rusks with Brown Butter and Herbs

SKORPOR

NUT-FREE, EGG-FREE, VEGETARIAN

MAKES: 32 rusks

PREP TIME: 30 minutes, plus 1½ hours to rise

COOK TIME: 30 minutes, plus several hours to crisp up in the oven with the heat off

8 tablespoons (1 stick) butter

1 cup milk

1 packet (2¼ teaspoons) active dry yeast

½ teaspoon sugar

2 cups all-purpose flour

1 cup whole-wheat flour

1 tablespoon chopped fresh rosemary

2 teaspoons fresh thyme leaves

2 teaspoons salt

½ teaspoon garlic powder

1. In a small saucepan, melt the butter over medium-high heat. Keeping a constant watch, allow the butter to turn golden brown, then add the milk. Heat until the mixture reaches 110°F. Put the yeast and sugar in a mixing bowl and pour over ½ cup of the mixture to dissolve it, letting it proof until it bubbles, 5 to 10 minutes. Stir in the flours, rosemary, thyme, salt, garlic powder, and remaining milk and butter mixture.

2. Knead the dough on a very lightly floured surface for about 5 minutes, then transfer to a bowl and cover with a clean tea towel to let rise for about 1 hour. Divide the dough in half and form each portion into a log about 16 inches long. Place the logs on a parchment-paper-lined baking sheet, cover them with the tea towel, and let rise for another 30 minutes.

3. Preheat the oven to 425°F. Bake for about 12 minutes, or until golden. Remove the baking sheet from the oven and allow the breads to cool for about 10 minutes, leaving the oven on for the next step.

4. When the breads are cool enough to handle, cut each log into 16 equal pieces. Arrange the slices in even layers on two large baking sheets. Bake for about 5 minutes, or until the slices begin to turn a toasty golden color. Flip the rusks, turn off the oven, and let them dry out in the oven with the door open for several hours or overnight.

This recipe is a celebration of my children's Scandinavian and English heritages. While these are not entirely authentic to one country, I'm delighted to have come up with a way to pair my husband's British roots with my own Norwegian heritage by subbing the meat in a British sausage roll with a spiced pork mix based on *medisterkaker*, which are fatty pork patties seasoned with nutmeg and ginger. The results are packed with flavor and totally irresistible.

Spiced Pork Sausage Rolls with Caramelized Onions

MEDISTERKAKER I BUTTERDEIG

NUT-FREE

MAKES: 4 to 6 servings
PREP TIME: 40 minutes
COOK TIME: 25 minutes

1 sheet frozen puff
   pastry (8 ounces)

1 pound ground pork

¾ teaspoon salt

¼ teaspoon ground ginger

⅛ teaspoon ground nutmeg

¼ cup milk

1 tablespoon butter

1 medium onion, sliced

2 tablespoons red wine

Pinch salt, for seasoning

1 egg, lightly beaten

Whole-grain mustard,
   for serving

1. Preheat the oven to 400°F. Set the puff pastry on the counter to defrost until it's workable but still cold, about 30 minutes.

2. Meanwhile, in a medium bowl, mix the pork, salt, ginger, and nutmeg with your hands until everything is just incorporated. Add the milk a little at a time, mixing until the mixture is soft; you may or may not need the entire amount. Take care to not overwork the meat.

3. In a skillet, melt the butter, then add the onion. Cook over medium heat for 20 minutes or so, stirring frequently, until the onion is caramelized. Add the wine and salt, stirring until the wine evaporates.

4. When the puff pastry is still cold but pliable, roll it out on a floured surface to an approximately 16-by-10-inch rectangle. Cut the rectangle in half lengthwise. Divide the pork in half and form each portion into a log. Place the meat logs lengthwise in the center of the pastry, and top with the caramelized onions.

5. Roll the pastry around the meat and brush the egg along the log to seal it closed. Brush the top of the pastries with egg, too, then score the tops about 1½ inches apart.

6. Cut each log into 4 equal pieces and place them on a large rimmed baking sheet. Bake until the pastry is golden brown and the meat is cooked through, about 25 minutes. Serve with mustard.

DID YOU KNOW? *Medisterkaker* (the spiced pork meatballs with gravy that inspired this recipe) are common elements of traditional Norwegian Christmas feasts. On holiday tables, the meatballs might nestle against a clove-studded roast pork belly known as *ribbe* and a variety of Nordic sausages (*pølser*), served with potatoes and a vinegar-based cabbage dish reminiscent of sauerkraut. You can find a number of Scandinavian Christmas recipes on my blog, *Outside Oslo* (www.outside-oslo.com).

Cured, smoked, sashimi-style, or grilled—I love salmon in all forms. Each holiday season, I try to make at least one batch of sweet-and-salty *gravlax* to serve to guests. It's an impressive yet deceptively easy way to share a little Scandinavian elegance with others. Throughout the year, I also frequently buy packages of smoked wild salmon to tuck into my kids' lunchboxes or add to a breakfast spread. Whether you use *gravlax* or smoked salmon, these puff pastry tarts are like Scandinavian *croque madames* and are an easy way to extend some Scandinavian-inspired hospitality to those you love.

Smoked Salmon Tarts with Potatoes, Eggs, and Herbs

LAKS TERTE

NUT-FREE

MAKES: 4 servings
PREP TIME: 15 minutes
COOK TIME: 25 minutes

1 sheet frozen puff
  pastry (8 ounces)

Olive oil, for brushing

4 medium Yukon Gold pota-
  toes, very thinly sliced,
  ideally with a mandoline

Salt, for seasoning

8 ounces shredded
  mozzarella cheese

2 Roma tomatoes, cut in
  half and sliced, or 6 cherry
  tomatoes, halved

4 eggs

4 ounces thinly sliced gravlax
  or smoked wild salmon

Dill or other herbs, for garnish

Microgreens, for
  garnish (optional)

Whole-grain mustard,
  for serving

1. Preheat the oven to 400°F. Line a baking sheet with parchment paper. Set the puff pastry on the counter to defrost until it's workable but still cold, about 30 minutes.

2. Roll out the pastry sheet to a 12-by-16-inch rectangle. Cut it into rectangular quarters, then fold the edges of each over ¼ inch to create a rim. Place the pastry pieces on the baking sheet about 1½ inches apart and prick them all over with a fork. Brush with olive oil. Arrange the potato slices over each of the pieces, avoiding the rim. Brush the potatoes with a little more olive oil and sprinkle with salt.

3. Bake for 10 to 12 minutes, or until the pastry has puffed and just begun to turn gold. Remove from the oven and sprinkle about half the cheese over the potatoes. Arrange the tomato slices on top, leaving a space in the center for an egg. Top the tomatoes with the remaining cheese. Crack an egg into the center of each pastry and sprinkle with salt, then return to the oven. Bake for 12 to 15 minutes, or until the cheese is melted and the eggs are cooked to your liking.

4. Arrange the salmon on the tarts and sprinkle with fresh dill and microgreens (if using). Serve with mustard.

Variations of this quiche or savory pie are usually made with Västerbotten cheese, a hard cow's cheese made in the north of Sweden. As I have trouble finding it—even in Seattle, where we have a well-stocked Scandinavian store in my neighborhood—I use extra-sharp Cheddar for this recipe with excellent results. This pie often appears at the *kräftskivor*—Swedish crayfish parties—that take place each August.

Mushroom and Cheese Quiche

SVAMP OCH VÄSTERBOTTENPAI

NUT-FREE, VEGETARIAN

MAKES: 1 (11-inch) pie
PREP TIME: 25 minutes, plus time for the dough to chill
COOK TIME: 1 hour 15 minutes

FOR THE CRUST

1 cup all-purpose flour

½ cup dark rye flour

9 tablespoons cold butter, cubed

½ teaspoon salt

7 tablespoons ice water

FOR THE FILLING

2 tablespoons butter

6 ounces cremini mushrooms, trimmed and thinly sliced

4 eggs

10 ounces aged Cheddar, shredded

¾ cup milk

1. To make the crust: Place the flours, butter, and salt in a food processor and pulse until crumbly. Add as much of the ice water as necessary and continue to pulse to make the dough come together, taking care to not overwork it. Gather the dough into a disk and wrap it in plastic. Refrigerate for 1 hour.

2. Preheat the oven to 375°F.

3. Roll the dough out on a lightly floured surface until it's a circle 12 to 13 inches in diameter. Transfer to an 11-inch tart pan with a removable bottom and press it in evenly. Line the dough with a sheet of parchment paper or foil, then fill with pie weights or dried beans to weigh down the dough as it bakes. Bake for 15 to 20 minutes, or until the crust begins to brown, then remove the weights, prick the bottom of the crust, and continue to bake for another 10 to 12 minutes, or until the bottom is golden.

4. Meanwhile, to make the filling, in a large skillet, melt the butter. Add the mushrooms and sauté over medium-high heat for 5 minutes, or until they've softened up a bit. Spoon the mushrooms evenly over the crust.

5. In a large mixing bowl, beat the eggs, then stir in the cheese and milk. Pour this mixture over the mushrooms in the crust. Bake until golden and set, about 25 minutes.

6. Let the quiche cool to room temperature to serve it the authentic Swedish way.

This silky vegetable-studded dish is a riff on the baked pancakes that can be found throughout Scandinavia. They are sometimes sweet and other times savory, as in *flaskpannkaka*, which is made with bacon. This one is hearty brunch fare, loaded with vegetables and herbs. Round out each plate with a generous serving of salad with mixed greens and herbs—oh, and perhaps a glass of something bubbly—and you'll be set. It's the sort of thing you'll be pleased to serve to your guests, knowing they'll be delighted by the taste and will leave nourished as well. The ultimate in Scandinavian hospitality.

Savory Baked Pancake with Vegetables and Herbs

■■ UGNSPANNKAKA

NUT-FREE, VEGETARIAN

MAKES: 4 servings
PREP TIME: 15 minutes
COOK TIME: 40 minutes

1 medium zucchini (9 ounces)

6 cremini mushrooms, destemmed

3 tablespoons butter, melted

2 cups milk, divided

3 eggs

1 cup all-purpose flour

½ teaspoon salt

1 tablespoon chopped fresh rosemary

1 teaspoon chopped fresh thyme

1. Preheat the oven to 425°F.

2. Cut the zucchini lengthwise and then into ¼-inch-thick slices. Cut the mushrooms into ¼-inch-thick slices as well.

3. Place the butter in a 12-by-9-inch baking dish, and swirl it around to coat the bottom of the dish. Arrange the zucchini and mushrooms in an even layer across the bottom of the dish. Bake for 10 minutes.

4. Meanwhile, in a mixing bowl, whisk together 1 cup of milk, the eggs, flour, and salt. When the mixture is smooth, add the remaining 1 cup of milk and whisk to combine.

5. Remove the pan from the oven. Sprinkle the herbs over the vegetables, then pour the batter into the pan, taking care not to disrupt the placement of the vegetables too much. Return the pan to the oven and bake for about 30 minutes, or until the cake is golden on top and set throughout.

VARIATION: Make this dairy-free and gluten-free by using almond milk and vegetable oil instead of the dairy milk and butter, and swapping out the flour for your favorite gluten-free variety.

THREE

Coffee Breads and Pastries

I USED TO KEEP AN EMPTY SPICE JAR in my office. It had previously contained cardamom, that exotic spice said to have made its way to the Nordic countries during the age of the Vikings. Each time I unscrewed the cap, a whiff of nostalgia overtook me as I thought of my Norwegian grandparents, long since departed, and I welcomed the tender memories the scent evoked.

Cardamom holds a prominent place in the food experiences of many Scandinavians, and it makes a frequent appearance in this chapter, from buttery buns to heart-shaped waffles. As you bake your way through these recipes, your home will be warm with the welcoming aromas of cardamom and cinnamon, vanilla, butter, and yeast. If there's one chapter that embodies a sense of *hygge*, it might just be this one.

It often smells like the neighborhood Scandinavian bakery in my home, with the aromas of freshly baked cardamom buns and hot coffee brewed as strong and dark as the Nordic night. No matter when in the day I make these buns, my children can smell them from the driveway when we get home from picking them up at school—a sweet surprise after a long day.

Classic Cardamom Buns
HVETEBOLLER/KARDEMOMMEBOLLER/VETE DEGBULLAR/ FØDSELSDAGSBOLLER

NUT-FREE, VEGETARIAN

MAKES: 12 buns
PREP TIME: 1 hour, plus about 1 hour 20 minutes to rise
COOK TIME: 30 minutes

1½ cups milk, divided

4 cups all-purpose flour, divided

8 tablespoons (1 stick) butter

2 teaspoons freshly ground cardamom

1 packet (2¼ teaspoons) active dry yeast

¾ cup sugar, divided

1 egg

½ teaspoon salt

1 beaten egg, for brushing

1. Measure out ⅔ cup of milk and ¼ cup of flour and set them aside—you'll need these in just a minute to make the roux/slurry for the *tangzhong* mixture (see Did You Know? on the next page).

2. In a medium saucepan, melt the butter over medium-high heat, then pour in the remaining ⅓ cup of milk and let it scald. Remove the pan from the heat and stir in the cardamom; let steep until the milk cools to lukewarm (110°F).

3. Meanwhile, in a small saucepan, combine the reserved ⅔ cup of milk and ¼ cup of flour and heat over medium to medium-high heat until the mixture thickens and pulls away from the sides of the pan. Remove the pan from the heat and let the mixture cool to lukewarm.

4. Place the yeast and 1 teaspoon of the sugar in a large mixing bowl. Pour a bit of the lukewarm cardamom milk over the yeast, stir, and let proof until the yeast bubbles, 5 to 10 minutes. Stir in the cooled roux, the remaining cardamom milk, the remaining sugar, the unbeaten egg, and the salt.

5. Stir in the remaining flour. Knead on a lightly floured surface for 10 to 15 minutes, taking care to not add too much flour. It will be somewhat sticky, but a bench scraper will help lift it off the counter while you work.

CONTINUED

Form the dough into a ball and let it rise in a lightly greased mixing bowl, covered with a clean tea towel, until doubled, about 1 hour.

6. Preheat the oven to 425°F. Line two baking sheets with parchment paper.

7. Punch down the dough and shape it into 12 equal balls, placing them on the baking sheets with the smoothest sides up. Cover with a damp towel and let rise for about 20 minutes.

8. Brush the tops of the buns with the beaten egg. Bake in the center of the oven, one sheet at a time, for 10 minutes, or until golden on top and baked through. (If the buns darken too quickly but still need more baking time, cover them with a sheet of aluminum foil.)

9. Cool completely on a wire rack before serving.

VARIATION TIP: Make these into *rosinboller*—Norwegian raisin buns—by folding in a cup or so of raisins at the end of kneading.

SERVING TIP: These buns are excellent smeared with butter and topped with paper-thin slices of *geitost* or *brunost*, the iconic Norwegian brown goat cheese with a somewhat sweet, caramel-like flavor and creamy texture. Find it at some grocery or specialty stores or online (see Resources, page 124). Look for "*Ekte Geitost*" from Tine or a pure goat cheese that does not also contain cow milk. While you're at it, consider buying an *ostehøvel*, a Norwegian cheese slicer.

DID YOU KNOW? While many homemade buns and breads are best the day they're made, the Asian technique known as the *tangzhong* method helps give them a little extra life. By making a roux of sorts with some of the flour and liquid, the dough can actually handle a higher hydration level, making it extra fluffy and able to stay fresh-tasting for days.

These *semlor* are over the top—which makes sense, considering their history as an indulgent pre-Lent treat. In this recipe, cardamom buns are stuffed with an almond filling and topped with mounds of sweetened whipped cream. Scandinavians enjoy *semlor* so much that, these days, they're not only served during Shrovetide (aka Pre-Lenten season), but through the months of January and February as well.

Shrove Tuesday Buns with Almond Paste and Cream

SEMLOR/FASTELAVNSBOLLER

VEGETARIAN

MAKES: 12
PREP TIME: 1 hour 10 minutes, plus about 1 hour 20 minutes to rise
COOK TIME: 40 minutes

FOR THE BUNS

1 recipe Classic Cardamom Buns (page 41)

FOR THE ALMOND FILLING

1 cup blanched almonds

½ cup confectioners' sugar

3 tablespoons milk or cream

½ teaspoon almond extract

FOR THE WHIPPED CREAM

2 cups heavy cream

¼ cup confectioners' sugar

½ teaspoon vanilla extract

FOR DECORATING

Confectioners' sugar, for dusting

1. Bake the cardamom buns as directed.

2. When they are cool, use a sharp knife to remove the tops. Scoop out part of the inside of each bun to use in the almond filling. Set aside.

3. To make the almond filling, whirl the almonds in a food processor until they're coarsely ground, then add the confectioners' sugar and reserved bun filling and pulse until combined. Pour in the milk, along with the almond extract, and continue to process until it comes together.

4. To make the whipped cream, in a mixing bowl, vigorously beat the cream until it thickens. Add the confectioners' sugar and vanilla extract and continue to beat until stiff peaks form.

5. Tuck the almond filling into the cavities of the buns, then pipe on a generous amount of whipped cream. Top with the lids of the buns, dust with confectioners' sugar, and serve.

TECHNIQUE TIP: When removing some of the interior of the bun, feel free to use your fingers, but I find it easiest to cut a circle with a knife and scoop out the bread with a grapefruit spoon.

I love baking Scandinavian buns any time of the year, especially in autumn when the days shorten and the weather cools. The scent of sweet yeasted dough, hot in the oven—especially when fragrant with spices like cinnamon and cardamom—creates a warm, welcoming touch to the kitchen. It's one of my favorite ways to create a sense of *hygge* in my home. It's apropos, then, that these *skoleboller*—or school buns—have a history of finding their way into Norwegian children's lunchboxes.

Sweet "School Buns" with Custard and Coconut

SKOLEBOLLER/SKOLEBRØD

NUT-FREE, VEGETARIAN

MAKES: 12

PREP TIME: 1 hour 10 minutes, plus about 1 hour 20 minutes to rise

COOK TIME: 10 minutes

1 recipe Classic Cardamom Buns (page 41), prepared through step 7

½ recipe Vanilla Pastry Cream (next page)

1 egg, beaten

FOR THE ICING AND TOPPING

2 tablespoons whole milk

1 cup confectioners' sugar

1 tablespoon butter, melted

¼ teaspoon vanilla extract

Unsweetened shredded coconut, for topping

1. Make the buns and pastry cream as directed.

2. Preheat the oven to 425°F. Line two baking sheets with parchment paper.

3. After the 12 buns have completed their second rise, use your thumb or a small spoon to make a depression in each ball and spoon in a tablespoon of the pastry cream. Brush with the beaten egg.

4. Bake in the center of the oven, one sheet at a time, for about 10 minutes, or until golden on top—watch carefully as they can quickly turn too dark. Rotate if needed for even baking. If they're browning too quickly and the insides need additional time, cover the tops with a sheet of foil. Remove the buns from the oven and let them cool completely on a wire rack.

5. While the buns cool, make the icing. In a medium bowl, gradually whisk the milk into the confectioners' sugar until you have a smooth, thick icing. Stir in the melted butter and vanilla extract.

6. Brush the top of each bun, around the pastry cream, with the icing, then dip in the dried coconut. Set aside to dry, then serve.

STORAGE TIP: As with many homemade buns, these are best on the day they come out of the oven. They also freeze well.

A luscious pastry cream is an essential recipe in a Scandinavian baker's reper- toire, and this is mine. You'll use it in a number of recipes throughout this book. You'll often have extra pastry cream left over. Keep it refrigerated, and over the next few days you'll be ready to assemble a quick trifle for an impromptu dessert—or simply serve it with fresh fruit.

VANILLA PASTRY CREAM

GLUTEN-FREE, NUT-FREE, VEGETARIAN

MAKES: 2 cups

2 cups whole milk

½ cup sugar

3 large eggs

3 tablespoons cornstarch

⅛ teaspoon salt

1 tablespoon butter, at room temperature

1 teaspoon vanilla extract

1. Find a bowl large enough to hold the saucepan you'll be using, and prepare an ice bath.

2. In the saucepan, bring the milk to a simmer and then immediately remove it from the heat.

3. In a medium bowl, vigorously whisk the sugar and eggs together for a minute or two, or until the sugar begins to dissolve. Stir in the cornstarch and salt.

4. To temper the eggs, slowly stream ½ cup of hot milk into the bowl with the sugar and egg mixture, whisking con- stantly. Then, slowly pour this mixture into the saucepan with the remaining milk and return the pan to medium heat, whisking constantly until the mixture thickens.

5. Add the butter and immediately transfer the pan to the prepared ice water bath, continuing to whisk until the butter melts. Stir in the vanilla.

6. Transfer the pastry cream to a bowl, cover with plastic wrap, and refrigerate until chilled.

Fragrant with the warm aromas of cinnamon, freshly ground cardamom, and hot, buttery yeasted dough, these buns are the epitome of Scandinavian coziness. They are a favorite recipe on my blog, and I've given them an update here with the *tangzhong* method of bread baking (see Did You Know? on page 42). Variations of these buns are popular throughout Scandinavia, and rightfully so. They seem—at least to me—like *hygge* or *koselig* in edible form.

Cinnamon and Cardamom Twists

KANELBULLAR/KANELSNEGL/KANELSNURRER

NUT-FREE, VEGETARIAN

MAKES: 16
PREP TIME: 30 minutes, plus about 1½ hours to rise
COOK TIME: 40 minutes

FOR THE DOUGH

1 cup plus 3 tablespoons whole milk, divided

3 cups all-purpose flour, divided

5 tablespoons butter

1 packet (2¼ teaspoons) active dry yeast

3 tablespoons sugar, divided

1 egg, at room temperature, lightly beaten

2 teaspoons freshly ground cardamom

1. Measure out ½ cup of milk and 3 tablespoons of flour and set aside—you'll need these in just a minute.

2. In a medium saucepan, melt the butter over medium-high heat, then pour in the remaining ½ cup plus 3 tablespoons of milk and let it scald. Remove from the heat and let the slurry cool until lukewarm (110°F).

3. While the milk cools, in a small saucepan, combine the reserved ½ cup of milk and 3 tablespoons of flour and cook over medium to medium-high heat until the mixture thickens and pulls away from the sides of the pan. Remove the pan from the heat and let it cool.

4. Place the yeast and 1 teaspoon of sugar in a large mixing bowl. When the butter and milk mixture is lukewarm, pour a little of it over the yeast and sugar in the bowl. Give it a quick stir, then let it sit until the mixture bubbles, 5 to 10 minutes. Add the cooled slurry, beaten egg, remaining sugar, and the cardamom. Gradually stir in the remaining flour.

5. Knead the dough on a lightly floured surface for about 10 minutes, or until the dough comes together and you can see little pockets of air if you cut into it. (The dough will be somewhat sticky—a bench scraper will help with this, but feel free to add a little more flour if needed.) Transfer to a large bowl, cover with a damp tea towel, and let rise until doubled, about 1 hour.

FOR THE FILLING

6 tablespoons butter, at room temperature

3 tablespoons packed brown sugar

1 tablespoon cinnamon

2 teaspoons freshly ground cardamom

FOR THE TOPPING

1 beaten egg, for wash

Scandinavian pearl sugar (optional but highly recommended), for sprinkling

6. Meanwhile, to make the filling, in a small bowl, mix the butter, brown sugar, and spices with a fork until smooth.

7. Roll out the dough on a lightly floured surface into a rectangle roughly 16-by-20 inches. Spread the filling over it, reaching all the way to the ends. With a long side facing you, fold the dough toward you, lengthwise, making a long, skinny rectangle about 8-by-20 inches. Cut the dough crosswise into 16 strips. Form each into a knot by twisting the ends in opposite directions a couple of times, then rolling them around your finger a couple of times and tucking in the ends. Place on baking sheets that are either greased or lined with parchment paper. Cover with damp tea towels and let rise another 30 to 60 minutes.

8. Preheat the oven to 400°F. Brush the twists with the beaten egg and sprinkle with pearl sugar, then bake for 10 to 12 minutes, rotating the pans and switching racks as needed for even baking.

DID YOU KNOW? Scandinavians love their cinnamon rolls so much that October 4 is the treat's official day. I think we'd all do well to adopt that holiday, don't you agree?

One of the notable qualities of Scandinavian baked goods is their tendency to be less sweet than their American counterparts. This cinnamon bun cake is an example. While it's loaded with a marzipan-based filling and pastry cream it somehow manages to stay balanced. I have, however, included an optional icing recipe—just in case you want to bump up the sweetness.

Almond-Filled Cinnamon Bun Cake

▰▰ ▰▰ BUTTERKAKA/SMORKAGE

VEGETARIAN

MAKES: 1 cake, plus a few additional rolls
PREP TIME: 50 minutes, plus about 1½ hours to rise
COOK TIME: 50 minutes

1 recipe Cinnamon and Cardamom Twists dough (page 46), prepared through step 5

½ recipe Vanilla Pastry Cream (page 45)

FOR THE REMONCE

7 tablespoons butter, at room temperature

3½ ounces marzipan

½ cup sugar

1 egg, beaten

Sliced almonds, for topping

1. Make the Cinnamon and Cardamom Twists dough, through the first rise as directed. Make the Pastry Cream as directed.

2. To make the *remonce*, in a small bowl, mix the butter, marzipan, and sugar with a fork until creamy.

3. Lightly grease or butter a large round cake pan (9 or 10 inches is ideal).

4. Roll out the dough on a lightly floured surface to a 12-by-16-inch rectangle. Spread with the *remonce*, then the pastry cream and roll lengthwise into a long log. Cut into 12 equal parts, then arrange them, cut-side up, about ½ inch apart in the pan, with one roll right in the middle—you'll only use about nine, depending on the size of your pan, but you can bake the remaining individually. Cover and let rise for 30 to 60 minutes, or until the buns have begun to stick together.

5. Meanwhile, preheat the oven to 400°F. Brush the tops with the beaten egg and scatter sliced almonds on top, then bake for about 20 minutes, or until golden brown and cooked through. Cool.

FOR THE ICING (OPTIONAL)

2 tablespoons water

1 cup confectioners' sugar

1 tablespoon butter, melted

¼ teaspoon vanilla extract

6. If you opt to make the icing, in a medium bowl, gradually add water by the teaspoon to the confectioners' sugar until you have a smooth, thick icing. Then stir in the melted butter and vanilla extract. Drizzle over the tops of the cakes—it's particularly pretty if you do this in a circle in the middle of each of the buns.

TECHNIQUE TIP: Get clean, neat rolls by slicing them with clean thread or unflavored dental floss instead of a knife.

VARIATION TIP: Change the flavor profile by substituting the cardamom and cinnamon filling from the Cinnamon and Cardamom Twists (page 46) for the one included here. They are both forms of *remonce*, a buttery mix that's used in many Danish pastries. The spiced one is called dark *remonce*, and you'll find a variation of it as the topping for *Brunsviger* in the next chapter. The version used in this recipe, made with marzipan, is light *remonce* (my favorite!); you'll also find it spread inside the flaky *kringle* on page 68 and the poppy- and sesame-seed coated *frøsnapper* on page 70.

Traditionally enjoyed on December 13 to celebrate St. Lucia's Day, these soft and buttery buns showcase the flavor of saffron, a very special and expensive spice used in a variety of Scandinavian baked goods. Be sure to try them with *gløgg* (next page) for the ultimate in holiday *hygge*.

Saffron-Scented St. Lucia Buns

▓▓ ▓▓ LUSSEKATTER/LUSSEBULLE

NUT-FREE, VEGETARIAN

MAKES: 32 buns
PREP TIME: 40 minutes, plus time for saffron to soak and 1 hour 30 minutes for the buns to rise
COOK TIME: 20 minutes

½ teaspoon saffron threads

1 cup sugar, divided

1 tablespoon whiskey or vodka

1 cup (2 sticks) unsalted butter

2½ cups milk

3 teaspoons active dry yeast

1 egg

1 teaspoon salt

8 cups all-purpose flour

1 beaten egg, for egg wash

64 currants or raisins

1. Prep the saffron the night before you're planning to bake: Crush it with 1 tablespoon of sugar in a small bowl. Stir in the whiskey and let it soak overnight, covered with plastic wrap, to let the alcohol draw out the saffron's color and flavor.

2. When you're ready to bake the next day, melt the butter in a medium saucepan. Pour in the milk and heat until it's scalded, then let it cool to lukewarm (110°F). Scoop out ½ cup or so and place in a bowl. Sprinkle the yeast over it, cover, and let it sit until it bubbles, 5 to 10 minutes.

3. In a large mixing bowl, beat one egg. Add the remaining sugar, the salt, the milk and yeast mixture, the remaining milk, and the saffron. Mix well with a wooden spoon. Gradually add the flour, thoroughly mixing as you go, until the dough comes together. (You may need slightly less than 8 cups of flour.)

4. Turn the dough out onto a lightly floured surface and knead for 5 to 10 minutes, or until it's light and elastic. (Take care to not add too much flour; this is a very sticky dough, and a bench scraper can help pull it from the surface while you work.) Return the dough to the mixing bowl and let rise in a warm place, covered with a clean tea towel, until doubled in size, about 1 hour.

5. Line 2 baking sheets with parchment paper. Cut the dough into 32 equal pieces and roll each into a log, working from the center out, until they're about the thickness of a finger. Form into "S" shapes by

COZY SPICED AND SPIKED MULLED RED WINE GLØGG / GLÖGG

GLUTEN-FREE, DAIRY-FREE, EGG-FREE, VEGAN

MAKES: 6 to 8 servings
PREP TIME: 15 minutes, plus time for spices to steep
COOK TIME: 30 to 45 minutes

1½ cups aquavit (or vodka or whiskey)

½ cup raisins

8 dried figs, quartered

3 cinnamon sticks

10 green cardamom pods

2 teaspoons whole cloves

1 star anise

2-inch piece of orange peel

1 (750 ml) bottle red wine, such as cabernet sauvignon

2 tablespoons sugar

¼ cup blanched almonds

Orange slices, for garnish (optional)

1. A day in advance, pour the aquavit into a jar along with the raisins, figs, cinnamon sticks, cardamom pods, cloves, star anise, and orange peel. Cover and let steep overnight, swirling it occasionally.

2. After about 12 hours, strain the mixture, reserving both the spiced aqavit as well as the spices, raisins, and figs until you're ready to make the *gløgg*.

3. When ready to heat the *gløgg*, in a medium saucepan, combine the spice-infused aquavit, reserved spices, raisins and figs, the wine, sugar, and almonds over low heat. Cover and let it slowly warm up for about 30 minutes or so, stirring occasionally. (There's a moment in which the *gløgg* goes from good to amazing—it's hard to describe until you've tasted it, but once you have you'll know what I mean.) Be patient and keep a gentle heat—you don't want the wine to boil, or even really simmer.

4. When the *gløgg* is hot and the flavors have developed to your liking, ladle it into mugs, ideally something clear and heatproof. Add raisins, figs, and almonds to each mug. Garnish with a cinnamon stick and slice of orange, if you wish.

simultaneously coiling each end in opposite directions. Place the buns on the baking sheets, then cover with a damp tea towel and let rise again for 30 minutes.

6. Preheat the oven to 400°F. Brush the buns with the egg wash. Press currants into the crevices of each "S," two per bun. Bake for 8 to 12 minutes, or until golden yellow on top and just cooked through. Slide the buns and the parchment paper they're on onto a wire rack and cover with another damp tea towel while they cool to keep them from drying out.

STORAGE TIP: Serve Lucia buns on the day that they're made, as they are prone to drying out quickly. If you have leftovers, they freeze well—just defrost them for a little bit and pop them back in the oven to reheat.

I've been savoring *julekake* for as long as I can remember, and the taste of it brings back a flood of memories and a sweet nostalgia for my childhood. I wish you could smell this buttery loaf that's fragrant with cardamom and studded with dried and candied fruits. Better yet, I encourage you to bake a batch and taste for yourself how incredible and special this bread is!

I found a recipe for *julekake* amid Grandma Adeline's extensive handwritten collection. She had written it out, in her neat, elegant script, between recipes for *rømmegrøt* (Norwegian sour cream porridge) and *lefse* followed by pumpkin chiffon pie (because she was American as well as Norwegian, after all). As I usually do, I've adapted the original to suit my tastes. It turned out just as I remembered it: warming, aromatic, festive, and just right for eating with thinly sliced *geitost*.

Christmas Bread with Raisins and Candied Fruit

🇳🇴 JULEKAKE

VEGETARIAN

MAKES: 2 loaves
PREP TIME: 1 hour, plus about 2 hours to rise
COOK TIME: 30 minutes

FOR THE BREAD

1 cup (2 sticks) butter

2 cups scalded milk

¼ teaspoon cardamom seeds, crushed

2 packets (4½ teaspoons) active dry yeast

⅔ cup sugar, divided

2 eggs, beaten

2 tablespoons grated orange zest

2 teaspoons salt

1 teaspoon cinnamon

6 cups all-purpose flour

1. To make the bread, in a small saucepan, melt the butter. Add the milk and scald. Remove from the heat and add the cardamom, letting the spice steep while the milk lowers in temperature to 110°F.

2. In a mixing bowl, combine the yeast with ½ teaspoon of the sugar and pour a little of the lukewarm milk over them. Let proof until it bubbles, 5 to 10 minutes.

3. Stir in the remaining milk, along with the eggs, remaining sugar, the orange zest, salt, and cinnamon. Add 5 cups of flour and gently mix, adding additional small amounts until the dough begins to pull away from the sides of the bowl. (You may not need to use the full 6 cups of flour.)

4. Transfer to a lightly floured surface and knead for about 10 minutes. Fold in the dried fruit and transfer to a lightly greased bowl. Cover with a clean tea towel and let rise until doubled, about 1 hour.

2 to 3 cups dried or candied fruit (raisins, candied fruit, chopped maraschino cherries)

1 beaten egg, for brushing

FOR THE ICING

2 cups confectioners' sugar

¼ cup whole milk

2 tablespoons butter, melted

½ teaspoon almond extract

FOR THE TOPPING

Sliced almonds

5. Punch down the dough and separate into two equal portions. You can either place them in two greased 9-inch round cake pans, or form them into two braided loaves. Cover with clean tea towels and let rise again until doubled, about 1 hour.

6. Preheat the oven to 375°F.

7. Brush the loaves with the beaten egg and bake for 30 minutes, or until golden. Cool on a wire rack.

8. When cooled, to make the icing, sift the confectioners' sugar into a medium bowl, then add the milk, melted butter, and almond extract and whisk until smooth. Drizzle over the loaves, then scatter the sliced almonds on top. Let set before slicing.

STORAGE TIP: Store extras wrapped in plastic at room temperature. When the bread starts to dry out, do yourself a favor and toast it, then smear it with butter, letting the butter melt into the cracks. Add *geitost*, too, if you have it. This is one of my favorite treats.

It's not often that one gets recipes passed down so many generations that they connect one's children with their great-great-grandmother. This recipe does that for me. I love inviting my kids to the kitchen counter when it's time to mix up a batch of waffle batter. Watching them help prepare a recipe that generations of women in my family have made fills me with joy every time. And I know that whenever they're eating a heart-shaped waffle, whether on a weekend or for an after-school treat, they're tasting the same sort of love that my mom and grandma gave to me each time they fed me. It's hard to imagine an heirloom much more valuable than that.

Great-Grandma Josephine's Heart-Shaped Waffles

VAFLER/VÅFFLOR

NUT-FREE, VEGETARIAN

MAKES: 6 servings
PREP TIME: 40 minutes, including time for the batter to rest
COOK TIME: 30 minutes

8 tablespoons (1 stick) butter, at room temperature

1 cup sugar

4 eggs

1 cup buttermilk

½ cup milk

2 cups all-purpose flour

¾ teaspoon freshly ground cardamom

½ teaspoon baking powder

½ teaspoon baking soda

1. In a large mixing bowl (ideally using a stand mixer), cream the butter and sugar together. Add one egg at a time, beating well and scraping down the sides as necessary. Mix in the buttermilk and milk. Add the flour, cardamom, baking powder, and baking soda, then mix into the batter to combine. Let the batter rest in the refrigerator for 30 minutes.

2. Meanwhile, preheat and lightly grease a heart-shaped waffle iron (or any waffle iron you have). To bake, measure about ⅓ cup of batter per waffle and bake according to the waffle maker's instructions.

VARIATION TIP: Cardamom is a typical flavoring for *vafler*, but if you don't mind veering from tradition, these are equally delicious flavored with vanilla and cinnamon. Simply swap out the cardamom for ¾ teaspoon of ground cinnamon and ½ teaspoon of vanilla.

TIP: *Vafler* are best, in my opinion, when they're made right after the batter is mixed. That way, they're fluffy from all that beating when you add the eggs. However, there's something cozy about the Norwegian habit of keeping a jug of batter in the fridge at the ready for whenever you want a snack or to serve a friend who stops by—or perhaps for an extra-special after-school snack for the kids. If you make the batter ahead of time, you'll just want to remove a portion of the batter from the fridge to warm up for a little bit before starting to cook the waffles.

DID YOU KNOW? If you're looking for an excuse to make waffles, mark your calendar for March 25, *Våffeldagen* (aka Waffle Day), a celebration that originated in Sweden. The same day is also Annunciation Day, commemorating the day Christians believe the angel Gabriel appeared to the Virgin Mary and told her she would give birth to Jesus. While there's nothing religious about the waffle celebration, *Våffeldagen* apparently sounds enough like *Vårfrudagen* (Our Lady Day) that it became its own thing.

SERVING IDEAS:

- Butter and jam (strawberry, raspberry, and lingonberry are popular choices)

- Sour cream topped with a dollop of strawberry jam

- Butter with a slice of *geitost* or *brunost*

- *Geitost* or *brunost* with a whisper-thin slice of white onion (I loved the combination of *geitost* and onion when I was growing up—my mom inherited the idea from her dad)

- Sprinkles over whipped cream and fresh raspberries (Yes, you read this right—I surprised my kids once with rainbow sprinkles on top of raspberry jam and they were delighted. Totally not traditional, and totally worth it.)

Much thinner than the pancakes that Americans slather with butter and maple syrup for brunch, these *pannekaker*—Norwegian pancakes—and their Swedish counterpart are more like crêpes. (While the Norwegian and Swedish versions are rather similar, *pannekaker* are a little thicker and eggier than *pannkakor*.) I've perfected my recipe over the years, and it's such a favorite in my home that I keep the recipe taped inside the cabinet above the mixer so it's always ready when I want to make a batch on a whim.

Pancakes with Blueberries and Bacon
PANNEKAKER MED BLÅBÆR OG BACON/PANNEKAKER/PANNKAKOR

NUT-FREE

MAKES: 2 to 3 servings
PREP TIME: 40 minutes, including time for the batter to rest
COOK TIME: 40 minutes

FOR THE PANCAKES

¾ cup all-purpose flour

1½ tablespoons sugar

1 teaspoon vaniljesukker (Scandinavian vanilla sugar, page 7) or vanilla extract

¼ teaspoon freshly ground cardamom (optional)

¼ teaspoon kosher salt

3 eggs

1½ cups whole milk

2 tablespoons unsalted butter, plus more for seasoning the pan

1. To make the pancakes, in a medium bowl, whisk the flour, sugar, *vaniljesukker*, cardamom (if using), salt, eggs, and milk until the batter is smooth. In a 10-inch cast iron pan that you'll eventually use to cook the pancakes, melt the butter and then pour it into the batter (the residual butter will prepare the pan for the first pancake). Refrigerate the batter for about 30 minutes while you prepare the blueberries and bacon.

2. To make the blueberry sauce, in a medium saucepan, combine the blueberries, water, sugar, and cinnamon and let simmer over medium heat for about 6 minutes, stirring occasionally. Add the sprig of thyme and continue to simmer until the sauce has thickened (increase the heat to medium-high if necessary). Remove the thyme.

3. To make the topping warm a large skillet over medium-high heat. Add the bacon and cook, turning every minute or so, for about 6 minutes, or until it's deeply golden brown and crisp. Transfer to a paper towel–lined plate to drain, then crumble into bite-size pieces when cool enough to handle.

FOR THE BLUEBERRY SAUCE

1 pint blueberries

½ cup water

1 tablespoon sugar

⅛ teaspoon cinnamon

1 small thyme sprig

FOR THE TOPPING

6 thick-cut bacon slices

Confectioners' sugar,
   for dusting

4. To cook the pancakes, warm the butter-coated cast iron pan over medium heat. Pour in enough batter to thinly coat the bottom of the pan—I find that a ⅓-cup measure is just right for my 10-inch pan. Twirl the pan around to coat the bottom, and when the top starts to set and the edges begin to color slightly, carefully but confidently and swiftly slide a spatula under the pancake, jiggling it slightly as you do, and flip the pancake. It will probably need about 2 minutes on the first side and a minute or so on the second. When done, use the spatula to roll or fold the pancake in the pan and transfer to a plate.

5. Repeat until you've used up all the batter, adding a little butter to the pan between pancakes if necessary. Cover the pancakes with a tent of aluminum foil as you go to keep them warm.

6. To serve, divide *pannekaker* between plates and spoon the blueberry sauce on top. Scatter the crumbled bacon over it, then dust with confectioners' sugar.

If cake pops married pancakes, these cakes—known as *munker* in Norway—are what you'd get. I've been trying to put my finger on exactly what the taste of *æbleskivers* evokes for me: Beignets? (Especially when dusted with confectioners' sugar.) Funnel cakes? Doughnuts? I suppose none of that really matters, because to most people with a family history of making *æbleskivers*, they taste like Christmas and camaraderie.

To make *æbleskivers*, you'll need a special pan—these are readily available online, as well as in specialty shops. I have a wooden-handled cast iron *æbleskiver* pan from Norpro that works great.

Doughnutty Pancake Puffs

▉▉ ÆBLESKIVER/MUNKER

NUT-FREE, VEGETARIAN

MAKES: 21 puffs
PREP TIME: 10 minutes,
plus 30 minutes for the
batter to rest
COOK TIME: 20 minutes

3 eggs, separated

1½ cups buttermilk

2 tablespoons sugar

1½ cups all-purpose flour

1 teaspoon salt

¾ teaspoon baking soda

¾ teaspoon baking powder

1 teaspoon vanilla extract

Unsalted butter, for the pan

1. In a mixing bowl, beat the egg whites until stiff peaks form.

2. In a separate mixing bowl, whisk together the buttermilk, egg yolks, and sugar. Add the flour, salt, baking soda, baking powder, and vanilla extract and continue whisking until there are no lumps.

3. Fold in the beaten egg whites. Let rest in the refrigerator for about 30 minutes.

4. Meanwhile, preheat the oven to warm. Heat a seasoned *æbleskiver* pan over medium-high heat. Melt butter in each well, using a pastry brush if needed to evenly grease each well.

5. Pour batter into each well, until they're two-thirds full, working clockwise and ending in the middle. Cook for a minute or two, then, working in the order in which you filled them, use a skewer or chopsticks to turn them, letting the uncooked batter spill out into the well to continue cooking. Some people simply flip

the *æbleskiver* to the opposite side, while others flip them about 90 degrees at a time, which yields a more spherical shape. When all sides are cooked, remove the *æbleskivers* to a plate and transfer to the oven to keep warm.

6. Brush more butter into each of the wells and repeat with the remaining batter.

TECHNIQUE TIP: To create filled *æbleskivers*, place some filling in the center of each *æbleskiver* right after you pour the batter into the pan, then top with more batter. Let cook for a minute or two and then turn them carefully, allowing the uncooked batter to spill into the bottom of the well and start to create more of the crust. If you're new to making *æbleskivers*, I would recommend that you first get the hang of the technique with the basic batter before adding any fillings.

DID YOU KNOW? *Æbleskivers* translates to "apple slices," and that hints at their most historical filling. Today, apples are not a requisite ingredient for these puffy pancakes—indeed, *æbleskivers* can be served plain with jam (give lingonberry a try) and confectioners' sugar, or they can be filled with just about anything you want, from various fruit compotes or preserves to chocolate. Some people even serve them with savory filling.

Marzipan, marshmallows, and chocolate? How can things get any better? I first tasted a *flødeboller*—a chocolate-draped marshmallow with a marzipan or biscuit base—at a cooking demonstration led by Icelandic chef Gunnar Karl Gíslason when he came to the Nordic Culinary Conference hosted by the Nordic Museum in Seattle. I remember him including a bit of mushroom for flavor, which created the most lovely complexity to this Danish specialty. Mine doesn't contain any fungi, but I'd like to think the blueberries and spices add a nice touch.

Chocolate-Cloaked Blueberry Marshmallow Puffs with Spiced Blueberries

■■ FLØDEBOLLER

GLUTEN-FREE, DAIRY-FREE, EGG-FREE

MAKES: 20 puffs
PREP TIME: 1 hour, plus time to chill
COOK TIME: 30 minutes

FOR THE BASE

7 ounces marzipan

FOR THE MARSHMALLOW LAYER

3 packets gelatin

½ cup ice-cold water

½ cup blueberry jam

1¼ cups sugar

1 cup light corn syrup

¼ teaspoon salt

Confectioners' sugar, for dusting

1. Preheat the oven to 375°F. Line a baking sheet with parchment paper.

2. To make the bases, roll out the marzipan to a thickness less than ⅛ inch. Cut the marzipan into 20 circles about 1½ inches in diameter. (A cookie cutter works well for this.) Transfer them to the parchment paper and bake for about 6 minutes, or until golden. Slide the parchment paper onto a wire rack and let the bases cool until set. Slide the empty baking sheet into the refrigerator to chill.

3. To make the marshmallows, in a large mixing bowl (use the bowl for your stand mixer if you have one), dissolve the gelatin in the water. While the gelatin dissolves, place the jam in a saucepan along with the sugar, corn syrup, and salt and heat, stirring, until it reaches 240°F on a candy thermometer (this is the soft ball stage).

4. With the electric mixer running, carefully pour the hot syrup over the gelatin in a steady stream and whisk on high speed until the mixture thickens and about doubles in volume. This should take about 15 minutes, but monitor it closely.

FOR THE BLUEBERRY FILLING

½ cup blueberry jam

½ teaspoon cinnamon

¼ teaspoon cardamom

⅛ teaspoon nutmeg

½ teaspoon cornstarch

FOR THE CHOCOLATE LAYER

7 ounces bittersweet chocolate, chopped

1 to 2 tablespoons vegetable oil (optional)

5. Meanwhile, to make the blueberry filling, in a small saucepan, heat the blueberry jam, cinnamon, cardamom, and nutmeg until simmering. Add the cornstarch and continue to heat, stirring constantly, until thickened.

6. Line a baking pan with parchment paper, covering the bottom and sides, and then dust it with confectioners' sugar. Pour the marshmallow mixture into the pan and refrigerate for 1 hour. When set, use the tool from step 1 to cut the marshmallow into 20 circles 1 ½ inches in diameter.

7. To assemble, slide the parchment paper with the marzipan disks back onto the cold baking sheet. Spoon a little of the spiced blueberry filling in the center of each marzipan disk. Top with the marshmallow disks.

8. To temper the chocolate, melt half of it in a double boiler. Remove it from the heat and stir in the vegetable oil and the other half of the chocolate until it melts. Dip the marshmallow in the chocolate to coat all the way to the base. Let set before serving.

TIP: If you have excess marshmallow cream, make it into individual marshmallows to top the hot chocolate on page 69. Cover a baking sheet with parchment paper and sprinkle with confectioners' sugar. While it's still soft, spread the marshmallow mixture into an even layer and cover with more confectioners' sugar. Let sit at room temperature until set, several hours or overnight. Then cut and dust the additional surfaces with confectioners' sugar.

TECHNIQUE TIP: A microwave makes easy work of tempering chocolate. Place about two-thirds of the chocolate in a microwave-safe bowl and microwave it in short bursts, about 15 seconds at a time at first, then 5 seconds at a time as it gets close to totally melting, stirring after each time. Then, stir the remaining chocolate into the melted chocolate, a little at a time.

A staple in Danish bakeries, these iced, berry-filled treats have been called the Danish equivalent of the popular boxed toaster pastries found in American supermarkets—without all the high-fructose corn syrup, dyes, and preservatives, of course.

Glazed Raspberry Pastry Slices with Sprinkles

HINDBÆRSNITTER

VEGETARIAN

MAKES: 12 slices
PREP TIME: 1 hour 45 minutes, including chilling time
COOK TIME: 9 minutes

FOR THE PASTRY

2 cups all-purpose flour

¾ cup confectioners' sugar

8 tablespoons (1 stick) cold butter, cubed

1 egg

½ teaspoon almond extract

¼ teaspoon salt

¾ cup raspberry jam

FOR THE GLAZE

¾ cup confectioners' sugar

1 tablespoon water

½ teaspoon vanilla extract

FOR THE TOPPING

Sprinkles

1. To make the pastry, in a food processor, blitz the flour, confectioners' sugar, and butter until the ingredients crumble together. Add the egg, almond extract, and salt and continue to process until the dough just comes together. Divide the dough in two portions and form each into a rough rectangle. Flatten each piece into a 1-inch-thick rectangular blocks. Wrap the blocks in plastic and chill until they're very cold, at least 2 hours or overnight.

2. Preheat the oven to 350°F. Line two baking sheets with parchment paper.

3. Remove the dough from the fridge about 10 minutes before you begin. Roll each block of dough into a 6-by-12-inch rectangle, patching it as needed. (Hint: Roll the dough out on sheets of parchment paper, then all you'll need to do is slide the paper onto the baking sheets.)

4. Bake on the lined baking sheets for about 9 minutes, or until the edges of the rectangles are just barely beginning to turn golden. Slide onto the counter to cool.

5. Spread the jam on one of the rectangles, then top with the other.

6. To make the glaze, whisk the confectioners' sugar, water, and vanilla extract together until smooth. Spread on the top layer, then scatter sprinkles liberally across the top. Let set, then cut into 12 rectangles with a sharp knife.

Cherries and cream must be one of the most perfect flavor combinations. While these Danish confections require a number of steps, you can make them in stages over the course of a couple of days, assembling the medals just before serving.

Individual Cherry-and-Cream-Filled Medals

▉▉ MEDALJER

MAKES: 15 cakes

PREP TIME: 2½ hours, including time for the dough and pastry cream to chill

COOK TIME: 20 minutes

FOR THE COOKIES

2 cups flour

11 tablespoons cold butter, cubed

¾ cup confectioners' sugar

¼ teaspoon salt

1 egg

1 teaspoon vanilla extract

FOR THE FILLING

1 packet unflavored gelatin

¼ cup liquid from a jar of cocktail (maraschino) cherries

½ recipe Vanilla Pastry Cream (page 45), chilled

1 cup heavy whipping cream

1. To make the cookies, pulse the flour, butter, confectioners' sugar, and salt in a food processor until crumbly. Add the egg and vanilla extract and continue to process until the ingredients come together into a dough. Wrap in plastic and chill for at least 1 hour.

2. Preheat the oven to 400°F. Line two baking sheets with parchment paper. Roll the dough out about ⅛-inch thick. Cut into 30 (3-inch) rounds. (You'll want to work with one-third of the dough at a time, keeping the rest in the fridge while you work.)

3. Place the dough rounds on the prepared baking sheets and bake for 8 to 10 minutes, until they just begin to turn golden on the edges. Remove the cookies from the oven and let them cool completely on a wire rack.

4. Meanwhile, to make the filling, in a small heatproof bowl, stir together the gelatin and maraschino cherry liquid. Warm the mixture by microwaving it for 5 to 10 seconds or placing the bowl over a pot of simmering water; whisk until the gelatin dissolves. Transfer the gelatin mixture to a medium bowl and mix in the pastry cream.

1 cup confectioners' sugar

2 tablespoons whole milk

1 tablespoon butter, melted

¼ teaspoon almond extract

Red food coloring,
   for decorating

15 maraschino cherries

5. In a separate bowl, beat the heavy cream until stiff peaks form, then fold the whipped cream into the pastry cream mixture. Cover and refrigerate for 1 hour, or until firm, then transfer the filling to a pastry bag fitted with a star tip.

6. While the filling chills, to make the icing, in a medium bowl, whisk together the confectioners' sugar, milk, butter, and almond extract until smooth, then stir in a drop or two of red food coloring to hint at the cherry flavor in the filling.

7. Spread the icing on the top of half of the cooled cookies, not quite reaching the edges. These are the tops of the medals, so they should be pretty.

8. Place a maraschino cherry in the center of each of the remaining cookies, then pipe the chilled pastry cream mixture around and on top of the cherry. Top with the iced cookies. Serve immediately.

Close your eyes and imagine biting into layers of buttery pastry encasing a soft center oozing with slightly sweet strawberries. The flaky pastry and syrupy berries stick to your lips and you instinctively reach for a napkin to wipe off the errant crumbs. But it's pointless, as you're immediately on to your next bite. That's my experience anytime I eat pastries made with Danish pastry dough—they're that incredible.

Roasted Strawberry Danish Braid

■■ JORDBÆR WIENERBRØD

VEGETARIAN

MAKES: 2 braids
PREP TIME: 1 hour, plus time to chill
COOK TIME: 1 hour

1 recipe Danish Pastry Dough (next page)

1 recipe Vanilla Pastry Cream (page 45)

FOR THE ROASTED STRAWBERRY FILLING

2 pounds strawberries, large ones quartered, medium ones halved

2 tablespoons sugar

1 teaspoon vaniljesukker (page 7) or vanilla extract

FOR THE TOPPING

1 egg, lightly beaten with a little water

Pearl sugar, for coating

½ cup sliced almonds

1 recipe glaze from Glazed Raspberry Pastry Slices (page 62), optional

1. To make the filling, preheat the oven to 400°F. Line a rimmed baking sheet with parchment paper. Scatter the berries on the pan and sprinkle with sugar and *vaniljesukker*. Roast for 20 minutes, or until the berries have softened significantly and released their juices. Leave the oven. When cool enough to handle, tip the berries and juices into a bowl, using the parchment paper like a funnel. Drain out the liquid, reserving for another use (such as spooning over the waffles on page 54).

2. With the oven remaining at 400°F, line two rimmed baking sheets with parchment paper.

3. Divide the dough into two parts and roll each into a 6-by-12-inch rectangle and place on the baking sheets.

4. Leaving a 2-inch strip lengthwise down the middle, cut slanting strips about 1 inch apart on either side. Then fill the center with the pastry cream and the roasted strawberries. Fold the pastry over the filling, folding inward and crisscrossing while you work. Cover and let sit 15 to 30 minutes to puff up a bit. Brush with egg beaten with a little water. Sprinkle with pearl sugar and almonds.

5. Bake until golden brown, about 30 minutes. Let cool, then drizzle the glaze over the braids (if using).

DANISH PASTRY DOUGH WIENERBRØD

NUT-FREE, VEGETARIAN

MAKES: enough for 1 large kringle or 2 pastry braids

1 cup milk

1 packet (2¼ teaspoons) active dry yeast

¼ cup sugar, divided

1 egg

3¼ cups all-purpose flour

½ teaspoon salt

2 sticks cold unsalted butter, cut lengthwise into ¼-inch slices

1. Warm the milk to 110°F and pour it over the yeast and ½ teaspoon of the sugar. After it foams, add the egg, flour, the remaining sugar, and the salt. Knead a few minutes. Chill for 1 hour. Arrange butter slices next to each other between sheets of parchment and roll very thin, approximately 6-by-16 inches.

2. Roll out the chilled dough on a lightly floured surface into a 16-by-24-inch rectangle. Arrange the butter on one half of the dough, lengthwise, leaving space along the border. Fold the other half of the dough over this and press to seal well so no butter seeps out during baking. Fold into thirds (like a business letter), wrap in plastic, and refrigerate for at least 30 minutes.

3. Rotate 90 degrees from the position the dough had been in before chilling and repeat the process, rolling it out into a long rectangle and folding it into thirds, then refrigerating for an additional 30 minutes.

4. Do this once more. Refrigerate until you're ready to use the dough, once again making sure to give it at least 30 minutes to get the butter cold enough.

VARIATION TIP: While it's definitely worth making the full amount of the Danish pastry dough at once, feel free to freeze half if you only want to make one braid. You can use it later to make a half-portion of *kringle* (page 68) or a small batch of *frøsnapper* (page 70).

TIP: Be sure to use a rimmed baking sheet, in case the butter and berries break through the pastry.

DID YOU KNOW? What Americans know as Danishes are called Vienna bread, or *wienerbrød*, in Denmark. No matter what you call them, they're delicious.

Various types of this pretzel-shaped pastry exist throughout Scandinavia. The word *kringle* or *kringla* can refer to a pastry or a cookie, depending on the recipe and the family. While some make a version of soft cookies by the same name, I grew up associating the term with the flaky, buttery pastry made with layers of pastry and *remonce* studded with raisins. That pastry was ridiculously buttery and rich, and utterly amazing. Also, I snuck a recipe for homemade hot chocolate on the next page ostensibly because it is a typical accompaniment to *kringle*. But really, I just love sharing homemade hot chocolate with my kids.

Flaky Almond-Filled Pastry Pretzel

▪▪ KRINGLE

VEGETARIAN

MAKES: 1 large kringle, serving 20

PREP TIME: 1 hour, plus time to chill

COOK TIME: 30 minutes

1 recipe Danish Pastry Dough (page 67), chilled

FOR THE REMONCE

1 stick butter, at room temperature

7 ounces marzipan

1 cup sugar

FOR THE TOPPING

½ cup raisins

1 egg, lightly beaten

Pearl sugar, for topping

Sliced almonds, for topping

FOR THE ICING (OPTIONAL)

2 cups confectioners' sugar

4 tablespoons whole milk

2 tablespoons butter, melted

½ teaspoon almond extract

1. Make and chill the dough as directed.

2. To make the *remonce*, in a small bowl, mix the butter, marzipan, and sugar with a fork or with your hands until creamy.

3. Line a rimmed baking sheet with parchment paper. Roll out and stretch the dough into a skinny 6-by-48-inch rectangle. Spread the *remonce* lengthwise along one side, then sprinkle with the raisins and roll up the dough, sealing it.

4. Transfer the dough to the baking sheet and form it into a pretzel shape. Cover and let it rise for about 30 minutes.

5. Preheat the oven to 400°F.

6. Brush the *kringle* with the beaten egg, then sprinkle pearl sugar and almonds on top. Bake for 30 minutes, or until golden, then remove the baking sheet from the oven and let the pastry cool on the pan.

7. If you're using the icing, sift the confectioners' sugar into a medium bowl, then add the milk, melted butter, and almond extract and whisk until smooth. Drizzle over the *kringle*. Let set before slicing.

ORANGE-SCENTED HOT CHOCOLATE WITH ALMOND WHIPPED CREAM

GLUTEN-FREE, EGG-FREE, VEGETARIAN

MAKES: 2 servings
PREP TIME: 10 minutes
COOK TIME: 5 minutes

2 cups whole milk

3 tablespoons grated orange zest, plus more for dusting

2 tablespoons Dutch process cocoa powder, plus more for dusting

1 tablespoon maple syrup

2 ounces dark chocolate, chopped

Pinch salt, for seasoning

FOR THE WHIPPED CREAM

1 cup heavy whipping cream

2 tablespoons confectioners' sugar

¼ teaspoon almond extract

1. In a medium saucepan, heat the milk along with the orange zest over medium heat until it simmers. Pour it through a sieve to remove the zest, then return the milk to the pot and heat. Whisk in the cocoa powder and maple syrup. Add the chopped chocolate and stir until it melts.

2. To make the whipped cream, pour the heavy cream into a large bowl and beat it with a whisk until it thickens. Add the confectioners' sugar and almond extract and continue to beat until stiff peaks form.

3. Divide the hot chocolate between two mugs. Top with whipped cream. Dust with additional orange zest and cocoa powder.

VARIATION: Make this dairy-free and vegan by using your choice of nondairy milk for the hot chocolate. To make dairy-free whipped cream, chill a can of full-fat coconut milk in the refrigerator overnight. Separate the hardened cream from the liquid, and beat this hardened cream with the confectioners' sugar until stiff peaks form.

DID YOU KNOW? Hot chocolate and hot cocoa are not simply different ways of describing the same thing. Rather, they hint at how the beverage is made: Hot chocolate includes melted chocolate, while hot cocoa is made with cocoa powder.

TIP: Save yourself a potential oven catastrophe by using a rimmed baking sheet to catch any errant butter.

Last but not least, the final recipe in this trio of pastries using Danish dough is a classic in Denmark. Layers of pastry are filled with almond *remonce* and coated in seeds before being twisted into individual pastries. If you're short on time, feel free to give this recipe a try with store-bought puff pastry—just don't miss out on this special Danish treat.

Flaky Poppy-Seed and Almond Pastries

▐▌ FRØSNAPPER

VEGETARIAN

MAKES: 20 pastries
PREP TIME: 1 hour, plus time to chill
COOK TIME: 20 minutes

1 recipe Danish Pastry Dough (page 67), prepared through step 2

½ recipe remonce from step 2 of Flaky Almond-Filled Pastry Pretzel (page 68)

1 egg, lightly beaten

⅓ cup poppy seeds

⅓ cup sesame seeds

1. Prepare the pastry dough as directed.

2. While the dough chills, make the *remonce*.

3. Preheat the oven to 400°F. Line a baking sheet with parchment paper.

4. Roll out the dough into a long, 24-by-16-inch rectangle. Spread the *remonce* lengthwise along one side. Fold the other half over it and seal.

5. Glaze with the beaten egg and sprinkle with poppy seeds, covering the entire surface. Carefully flip and glaze the other side with egg, then cover with the sesame seeds.

6. Slice the dough crosswise into 20 strips. Twist each slice two times and place the twists on the prepared baking sheet. Cover and let rise for about 20 minutes.

7. Bake the pastries for about 20 minutes, or until golden.

For some reason, I didn't taste my first Napoleon Hat until I set about creating the recipe for this book. I was missing out. I encourage you to not make that same mistake. These decorative little pastries are eye-catching, sure, with their tricorne hat shape, but I love them most for their delicious flavor trio of almond paste, cardamom, and melted chocolate.

Chocolate-Dipped Almond Napoleon Hats

NAPOLEONSHATTE/NAPOLEONHATTAR

VEGETARIAN

MAKES: 12 pastries
PREP TIME: 2 hours, including time for the dough to chill
COOK TIME: 15 minutes

FOR THE FILLING

7 ounces almond paste, grated

¼ to ⅓ cup sugar

1 egg white

¼ teaspoon freshly ground cardamom

FOR THE PASTRY

1 recipe shortcrust pastry from the Raspberry Pastry Slices (page 62), chilled

FOR THE CHOCOLATE

7 ounces bittersweet chocolate, chopped

1 tablespoon vegetable oil

1. Preheat the oven to 350°F. Line a baking sheet with parchment paper.

2. In the small bowl of a food processor, mix the almond paste, sugar, egg white, and cardamom until smooth. Chill for about 15 minutes.

3. Remove the prepared dough from the fridge about 10 minutes before rolling. Roll it out to a little less than ⅛-inch thick and cut into a dozen 3-inch circles, placing them on the parchment paper.

4. Divide the chilled filling into 12 equal portions and form into rough balls (they'll be sticky), placing them on the center of each circle of dough.

5. To form the hats, gather up the dough around the filling in a triangular shape reminiscent of a tricorne hat.

6. Bake for 12 to 15 minutes, or until beginning to turn golden. Cool on a wire rack.

7. While the hats cool, to temper the chocolate, melt half of it in a double boiler. Remove from the heat and add the vegetable oil and the rest of the chocolate, stirring until melted. Dip the bottoms of each hat in the chocolate and let them set, upside down, on parchment paper.

FOUR

Cakes

LEMON-FLECKED SUNSHINE
CAKE with Blueberries and
Thyme-Scented Glaze 75

MARZIPAN-DRAPED PRINCESS
CAKE with Raspberries, Pastry
Cream, and Cream 76

STRAWBERRY-AND-CREAM
LAYER CAKE 78

CLASSIC RHUBARB CAKE with
Hints of Cardamom and Almond 81

BUTTERY CARAMEL AND ALMOND
TOSCA CAKE with Boozy
Cherries 82

CHOCOLATE- AND VANILLA-
SWIRLED TIGER CAKE 84

FUDGY CHOCOLATE CAKE 85

ANNA-LISA'S YEASTED
APPLESAUCE CAKE 86

   BONUS RECIPE: Apple
   Parfait with Spiced
   Bread Crumbs and Cream

ALMOND WREATH CELEBRATION
TOWER 88

RASPBERRY-FILLED CARDAMOM
AND ALMOND PRINCE CAKE 90

YEASTED BROWN SUGAR
AND BUTTER CAKE 92

ANNA-LISA'S CHEESECAKE 93

AFTER ALL OF MY GRANDPARENTS passed away, I—by default, being the food writer who had been collecting recipes of our Norwegian heritage—became the keeper of our family's culinary traditions.

While many of my Scandinavian baking memories extend well into the past, I'm actively working to keep them current. One way I do so is with birthday cakes. So far, I've made the birthday cakes for each of my children's birthdays (even though I often want to outsource the task), and by far, they request the Scandinavian ones more than any other

From the *kransekake* I famously flopped for my son's second birthday (it was my first try, but he exclaimed, "good cookie!" upon first taste, so I convinced myself to consider it a success) to the strawberry-and-cream layer cake I've made for my daughter over the years, the recipes in this chapter are some of my favorite ways to share the delicious flavors of my heritage with those I love.

Vibrant enough to match the sun at *midnattsol* (that time in the North when the sun does not set), this lemon-scented Norwegian sponge cake is perfect to pair with a cup of tea. While blueberries and thyme are not typical additions to this classic cake, I love the way all the flavors work together.

Lemon-Flecked Sunshine Cake with Blueberries and Thyme-Scented Glaze

SOLSKINNKAKE MED SITRON, BLÅBÆR OG TIMIAN

NUT-FREE, VEGETARIAN

MAKES: 1 (8-inch) cake
PREP TIME: 30 minutes
COOK TIME: 35 minutes

FOR THE CAKE

3 eggs

½ cup sugar

1½ cups all-purpose flour

1½ teaspoons baking powder

¼ teaspoon salt

8 tablespoons (1 stick) butter, melted

Grated zest of 1 lemon

2 teaspoons lemon juice

1 teaspoon vanilla extract

1 cup blueberries

FOR THE GLAZE

¼ cup lemon juice

1 tablespoon fresh thyme leaves

1¼ cups confectioners' sugar, sifted

2 tablespoons whipping cream

1. Preheat the oven to 350°F. Grease an 8-inch spring-form cake pan.

2. To make the cake, in a large mixing bowl, whip the eggs and sugar together until the eggs have tripled in volume; if you're using an electric mixer at high speed, this should take just a minute or two.

3. Sift the flour, baking powder, and salt together, then fold into the foam. Add the melted butter while the mixer is running. Add the lemon zest, lemon juice, and vanilla extract. Stir in the blueberries.

4. Pour the batter into the prepared pan. Bake for about 35 minutes, or until a toothpick inserted in the center comes out clean. Cool in the pan for about 15 minutes, then remove.

5. Meanwhile, to make the glaze, in a small saucepan, bring the lemon juice to a boil with the thyme. Immediately remove from the heat and allow to cool while the thyme infuses with the lemon juice. In a small bowl, whisk the confectioners' sugar, whipping cream, lemon juice, and thyme leaves until smooth. Poke holes all over the top of the cake. Use a pastry brush to spread the glaze over the cake, taking care to evenly distribute the thyme leaves.

This Swedish classic might be among the most iconic of Scandinavian cakes, with its bright green covering and layers of rich cake and filling.

Marzipan-Draped Princess Cake with Raspberries, Pastry Cream, and Cream

PRINSESSTÅRTA

NUT-FREE

MAKES: 1 (9-inch) cake

PREP TIME: 1 hour, plus an hour for the individual elements to chill, and another hour for the assembled cake to chill and set

COOK TIME: 1 hour

FOR THE CAKE

6 eggs, separated

½ teaspoon cream of tartar

1 cup sugar

1 cup cake flour

1 teaspoon baking powder

¼ teaspoon salt

FOR THE PASTRY CREAM

½ recipe Vanilla Pastry Cream (page 45), chilled

FOR THE STABILIZED WHIPPED CREAM

1 packet unflavored gelatin

2 tablespoons cold water

1 cup heavy whipping cream

3 tablespoons confectioners' sugar

1 teaspoon vanilla extract

1. Preheat the oven to 325°F. Line the bottom of a 9-inch springform pan with a circle of parchment paper and coat the paper with nonstick cooking spray.

2. In a mixing bowl, beat the egg whites with the cream of tartar until they're fluffy, then add the sugar and continue to beat until stiff. In separate bowl, beat the egg yolks. In yet another bowl, whisk together the flour, baking powder, and salt. Fold the egg yolks and the flour mixture into the egg whites. Pour the batter into the pan.

3. Bake for about 1 hour, or until the center springs back when you touch it. Set on a wire rack to cool, then unmold.

4. Make and chill the pastry cream as directed.

5. To make the stabilized whipped cream, soften the gelatin in the cold water for 5 minutes. Heat this for a few seconds in the microwave or over a double boiler—you just want it to liquefy. Use a chilled bowl to beat the cream using an electric mixer. When it begins to thicken, add the confectioners' sugar and vanilla extract. Continuing to beat, pour the softened gelatin into the cream in a thin stream and beat until stiff but still luscious and fluffy.

½ cup raspberry jam

14 ounces marzipan

Green food coloring

Confectioners' sugar,
   for dusting

6. To assemble, cut the cake into three horizontal layers using a long serrated knife. Place the bottom layer of cake on a cake tray. Spread it with the raspberry jam and then place the second layer on top. Cover this with the pastry cream, then top with the third layer of cake. Chill for at least 1 hour to give it time to set. Coat the top and sides of the cake with the whipped cream, generously piling more on top into a dome.

7. Knead the marzipan and green food coloring until the marzipan is a minty green color (reserve a little of the marzipan to tint pink, if you'd like to form a rose to top the cake). Roll out the marzipan on a surface lightly dusted with confectioners' sugar so it's a large circle, about ⅛-inch thick. Drape it over the cake and trim any excess or tuck it under the cake. Dust with confectioners' sugar.

TECHNIQUE TIP: Rolling out marzipan is similar to working with cookie dough. But instead of dusting your work surface with flour, you'll use confectioners' sugar. Form the marzipan into a ball, then roll it on your board, alternating directions frequently, until you have a thin circle large enough to drape over the cake. (Rough edges can be tucked under the cake after draping.)

Underneath the luscious whipped cream that tops this beauty, you'll find four layers of sponge cake nestled up with satiny pastry cream and strawberry jam, with plenty of berries tucked in. It's the essence of spring and summer in my home—and distinctly Norwegian. While there are variations of this cake, with different types of fruits, I'm loyal to the pastry-cream-and-strawberry profile I first encountered years ago. This has been my daughter's birthday cake on repeat, and it's a true favorite in my home.

Strawberry-and-Cream Layer Cake

BLØTKAKE

NUT-FREE, VEGETARIAN

MAKES: 1 (9-inch) cake
PREP TIME: 45 minutes
COOK TIME: 1 hour

1 recipe batter from Princess Cake (page 76), prepared through step 2

1 recipe Vanilla Pastry Cream (page 45), chilled

1 cup strawberry jam

½ pint strawberries, hulled and sliced, plus more for garnish

1 recipe stabilized whipped cream from Princess Cake (page 76)

1. Preheat the oven to 325°F. Line the bottom of two 9-inch round cake pans with parchment paper and coat the paper with nonstick cooking spray.

2. Make the cake batter and divide it between the prepared cake pans. Bake for about 1 hour, or until the centers spring back when you touch them. Transfer the cake pans to a wire rack to cool for a few minutes, then unmold the cakes onto the rack and let cool completely.

3. Make and chill the pastry cream as directed.

4. To assemble, place the bottom cake layer on a serving plate or cake stand. Spread ½ cup of strawberry jam, then half the pastry cream over this. Top with a second layer of cake. Spread another ½ cup of strawberry jam over this and cover with the sliced strawberries, working in a spiral from the outside in. Place another layer of cake over this, spread on remaining pastry cream, and top with the final layer of cake.

CONTINUED

5. Refrigerate the cake until you're ready to use it—even a day in advance. Make the stabilized whipped cream as directed.

6. To finish, spread or pipe the whipped cream over the top and sides of the cake. Decorate with additional strawberries.

TECHNIQUE TIP: One great thing about making *bløtkake* for a celebration is that it can be made ahead of time and refrigerated until you're ready to serve it. Just wait until right before your event to spread on the whipped cream.

Slicing stalks of rhubarb never fails to delight. I love the ombré nature of the slices when they're lined up by hue, and the tart, almost vegetal aroma is as intoxicating to me as the scent of buttery pastries still warm from the oven. I've been making variations of this classic Norwegian rhubarb cake for years, and it's one of my favorite recipes in my dessert repertoire.

Classic Rhubarb Cake with Hints of Cardamom and Almond

RABARBRAKAKE MED KARDEMOMME OG MANDEL

VEGETARIAN

MAKES: 1 (9-inch) cake
PREP TIME: 20 minutes
COOK TIME: 50 minutes

3 rhubarb stalks

1¾ cups all-purpose flour

2 teaspoons baking powder

½ teaspoon freshly ground cardamom

½ teaspoon kosher salt

1 cup (2 sticks) unsalted butter, at room temperature

¾ cup sugar

2 eggs

2 teaspoons vanilla extract (or 1 teaspoon vaniljesukker, page 7)

1 teaspoon almond extract

½ cup sliced almonds

Confectioners' sugar, for dusting

1 tablespoon turbinado or sanding sugar

Whipped cream, for serving (optional)

1. Preheat the oven to 350°F. Grease a 9-inch springform pan with cooking spray and line the bottom with parchment paper.

2. Cut half of the rhubarb stalks into ¼-inch slices on the diagonal and the other half into 3-inch lengths; set aside.

3. In a medium mixing bowl, whisk together the flour, baking powder, cardamom, and salt.

4. In a large mixing bowl, cream the butter and sugar until it's pale and mousselike, about 3 minutes, scraping down the sides of the bowl as needed. Add the eggs, mixing well. Stir in the vanilla extract and almond extract. Add the flour mixture and stir until incorporated. Stir in the rhubarb slices, then pour the batter into the prepared pan. Top with the remaining rhubarb lengths in a decorative design.

5. Bake for about 50 minutes, or until a toothpick inserted in the center comes out clean. Cool for about 5 minutes, then remove from the pan and continue cooling on a rack.

6. Scatter sliced almonds on top of the cake, dust with confectioners' sugar, and sprinkle with turbinado sugar. Serve with whipped cream if you wish.

VARIATION TIP: Substitute vegan butter for the butter and omit the whipped cream to make this recipe dairy-free.

When I began collecting Scandinavian cookbooks in my twenties, *The Great Scandinavian Baking Book* by Beatrice Ojakangas was one of the first I bought, and it's still among my favorites. Her recipe for Tosca cake—a buttery cake topped with crisp caramel and almonds—was exceptional. I've made variations over the years and have come up with my own ideal version, which includes rum-soaked cherries. It's an optional step to be sure, but one that elevates this already spectacular cake to something out of this world.

Buttery Caramel and Almond Tosca Cake with Boozy Cherries

TOSCAKAKE MED KIRSEBÆR

VEGETARIAN

MAKES: 1 (9-inch) cake, serving 8 to 10

PREP TIME: 1½ hours, including soaking time

COOK TIME: 35 minutes

FOR THE CAKE

2 cups pitted cherries (fresh or frozen)

½ cup rum or liqueur (kirsch, amaretto, whiskey, or brandy)

3 eggs

½ cup sugar

1½ cups all-purpose flour

1½ teaspoons baking powder

¼ teaspoon salt

8 tablespoons (1 stick) butter, melted

1 teaspoon vanilla extract

½ teaspoon almond extract

1. Preheat the oven to 350°F. Grease a 9-inch springform pan with cooking spray.

2. To make the cake, in a shallow bowl, let the cherries soak in the liquor, stirring occasionally, for an hour or so. (If you're using frozen berries, they can defrost in the liquor.)

3. Meanwhile, in a large mixing bowl, vigorously beat the eggs and sugar until frothy, about 3 minutes. Add the flour, baking powder, and salt and mix just until incorporated. Pour in the melted butter, vanilla extract, and almond extract and combine.

4. Pour into the prepared cake pan. Spoon the cherries out of the liquor, scattering them across the top of the cake. Press into the batter using the back of a spoon. (Reserve the liquor, which will now be infused with a deep cherry flavor, for another use—it makes a lovely drink when served over ice with sparkling water.)

5. Bake for about 35 minutes, or until a toothpick inserted in the center comes out clean.

FOR THE TOPPING

8 tablespoons (1 stick) butter

¾ cup sliced almonds

½ cup sugar

¼ cup whipping cream

6. A few minutes before the cake is done, to make the topping, in a small saucepan, melt the butter. Stir in the almonds, sugar, and cream and bring to boil, stirring constantly, about 3 minutes, or until thickened a bit, then pour it over the cake.

7. Return the cake to the oven, set it to broil, and broil until the topping is bubbling and turning golden. This should take about 2 minutes, but watch carefully as it will quickly turn dark. Cool in the pan.

Marbled cake can be found throughout the Nordic countries, as well as in other parts of the world. Baked in a loaf pan or a Bundt pan, it reveals swirls of chocolate and vanilla or citrus-flavored cake when sliced.

Chocolate- and Vanilla-Swirled Tiger Cake

TIGERKAKA/TIGERKAKE/MARMORKAGE

NUT-FREE, VEGETARIAN

MAKES: 1 loaf cake
PREP TIME: 45 minutes
COOK TIME: 1 hour

1 cup (2 sticks) butter, at room temperature, plus more for greasing the pan

1¼ cups sugar

4 eggs

1 teaspoon vanilla extract

2¼ cups cake flour, plus more for coating the pan

2 teaspoons baking powder

2 tablespoons natural, unsweetened cocoa powder

2 ounces semisweet chocolate, finely chopped

2 teaspoons instant espresso powder

¼ cup milk

1. Preheat the oven to 350°F. Butter and flour an 8½-by-4½-inch loaf pan.

2. In a large mixing bowl, cream the butter and sugar until light and fluffy. Add the eggs, one at a time, mixing well each time. Stir in the vanilla extract. Sift together the flour and baking powder and add to the batter. Stir just until incorporated. Set aside two-thirds of the batter.

3. To the remaining third of the batter, mix in the cocoa powder, chocolate, espresso powder, and milk.

4. Spoon about one-fourth of the reserved batter into the bottom of the loaf pan, spreading it out a bit with a spatula. Add a spoonful of the chocolate batter in the center. Repeat, alternating the layers, until you've used all of the batter.

5. Bake for about 1 hour, or until a toothpick inserted in the center comes out mostly clean. Let cool completely on a wire rack before serving.

As simple and quick as the recipe is to prepare, this fudgy cake is just as luscious as the flourless chocolate cakes and molten lava cakes on fancy restaurant dessert menus. Do yourself a favor and err on the side of underbaking this cake. If you overbake it, you'll end up with more of a brownie than a cake.

Fudgy Chocolate Cake

KLADDKAKA

NUT-FREE, VEGETARIAN

MAKES: 1 (9-inch) cake, serving 12
PREP TIME: 10 minutes
COOK TIME: 20 minutes

8 ounces bittersweet chocolate (I used 60 percent cacao)

1 cup (2 sticks) unsalted butter

1 teaspoon instant espresso powder

1 teaspoon vanilla extract

4 large eggs

1 cup sugar

2¼ cups all-purpose flour

1 teaspoon baking powder

Confectioners' sugar, for dusting

Sweetened whipped cream and fresh berries, or vanilla ice cream, for serving (optional)

1. Preheat the oven to 425°F. Grease a 9-inch springform pan with nonstick cooking spray.

2. Roughly chop the chocolate, using either a sharp knife or a food processor.

3. In a deep saucepan, melt the butter over medium heat. Remove from the heat and add the chocolate, stirring until melted. Stir in the espresso powder and vanilla extract. Set aside and let cool until lukewarm.

4. In a large mixing bowl, beat the eggs and sugar until frothy, then stir in the melted chocolate and butter. In another bowl, whisk the flour and baking powder to combine, then gently fold into the batter until incorporated.

5. Pour the batter into the prepared pan and bake for 14 minutes; you want it to be a little underbaked at this point. Cool in the pan on a wire rack—don't skip this step! Remove from the pan and dust with confectioners' sugar. Serve with sweetened whipped cream and fresh berries or a generous scoop of vanilla ice cream, if desired.

TECHNIQUE TIP: The magic in this cake is in the timing. There's no real way to guarantee that your timing is perfect until the cake has cooled and you've cut a slice. Go for the 14-minute bake time the first time around, and make a note if you need to give it a minute or two more or less the next time.

Like *brunsviger* (page 92), this is also a yeasted cake. I've adapted it quite a bit from my husband's great-aunt Anna-Lisa, who was a cooking teacher in Sweden and whose instructions only called for applesauce, likely assuming that one would start with something good. But do yourself a favor and don't skip the homemade applesauce—a store-bought version won't compare. Serve this cake warm with vanilla ice cream on a crisp autumn evening for a cozy, warming treat or, for pure apple indulgence, a classic Norwegian apple parfait with spiced bread crumbs and cream (next page).

Anna-Lisa's Yeasted Applesauce Cake

ÄPPELKAKA

NUT-FREE, VEGETARIAN

MAKES: 8 servings
PREP TIME: 65 minutes, including time for components to rise or chill
COOK TIME: 70 minutes

FOR THE APPLESAUCE

2 pounds apples, peeled, cored, and cut into 1-inch chunks

⅔ cup water

½ cup sugar

2 teaspoons cinnamon

½ teaspoon salt

FOR THE CAKE

14 tablespoons (1¾ sticks) butter

¼ cup milk

2 packets (4½ teaspoons) active dry yeast

2 tablespoons sugar

2 eggs

2 cups all-purpose flour

1. To make the applesauce, put the apples in a large pot along with the water, sugar, cinnamon, and salt and bring to a simmer over medium heat. Allow to cook, adjusting the heat as necessary to maintain a gentle simmer, until the apples are tender and beginning to fall apart, about 30 minutes. Remove from the heat, transfer to an airtight container and refrigerate until chilled.

2. To make the cake, in a small saucepan, melt the butter. Pour in the milk and let it cool to 110°F.

3. Pour a little of the lukewarm butter and milk over the yeast and sugar in a mixing bowl. Stir and let proof until it bubbles, 5 to 10 minutes. Stir in the eggs and the remaining butter and milk mixture, then the flour. Set this aside while you make the topping.

4. To make the topping, in a small saucepan, melt the butter and then stir in the sugar and vanilla extract.

5. Grease a 9-by-12-inch cake pan (feel free to use a comparable size pan here, adjusting the baking time as needed). Divide the dough into two parts, one a little smaller than the other (leave that one for the top). Press the larger portion across the bottom of the pan.

APPLE PARFAIT WITH SPICED BREAD CRUMBS AND CREAM
TILSLØRTE BONDEPIKER

NUT-FREE, VEGETARIAN

MAKES: 6 servings
PREP TIME: 30 minutes
COOK TIME: 45 minutes

4 tablespoons (½ stick) butter

3 tablespoons sugar

1 teaspoon cinnamon

¼ teaspoon salt

3 cups bread crumbs

2 recipes Applesauce
   (previous page)

1 recipe whipped cream
   from Shrove Tuesday
   Buns with Almond Paste
   and Cream (page 43)

1. In a large skillet, melt the butter. Stir in the sugar, allowing it to melt, then add the cinnamon and salt. Tip in the bread crumbs and stir frequently over medium-high heat, taking care that the sugar doesn't burn, until the bread crumbs are crisp. Cool until ready to use.

2. To assemble the trifles, layer the applesauce, whipped cream, and bread crumbs in individual glass bowls or one large one.

3. Garnish with mint leaves, rosemary sprigs, or a dusting of ground cinnamon or nutmeg.

TECHNIQUE TIP: To make your own bread crumbs for this recipe, pulse 3-inch portions of a stale baguette in a food processor.

VARIATION TIP: If you have any extra Vanilla Pastry Cream (page 45) from one of the other recipes, layer it along with the other ingredients for an over-the-top autumn dessert.

FOR THE TOPPING

5 tablespoons butter, at
   room temperature

⅓ cup sugar

1 teaspoon vanilla extract

1 egg, lightly beaten

Spread 1½ cups of the applesauce over the surface and top with the other portion of dough. Spread the butter topping over the top. Cover with a clean tea towel and let rise for 30 minutes.

6. Preheat the oven to 400°F. Brush the dough portions of the cake with the beaten egg. Bake for 20 to 25 minutes, depending on the size of your pan, until the top is golden and a toothpick inserted in the middle comes out clean.

7. Cool in the pan on a wire rack.

Kransekake is a traditional Norwegian and Danish celebration cake that's often served at weddings, birthdays, anniversaries, and other celebrations. I've always seen it in a tower constructed of incrementally smaller rings, but it can also take the shape of a horn to be filled with treats. While it's possible to see a *kransekake* decorated with restraint—with only the scalloped icing around each ring—this cake is typically decorated with Norwegian or Danish flags and other festive touches. It is, after all, a celebratory dessert, and the decorators often go all out to showcase this function.

While the results are impressive, the cake itself requires only a handful of ingredients and a set of *kransekake* cake forms, which you can find in Scandinavian specialty stores or online. I like to add a pinch of salt and boost the almond flavor with a little almond extract, but these additions are just a matter of taste.

Kransekake has a delightful texture—chewier than a cookie and light yet surprisingly sturdy, which is essential, as it needs to hold up to its towering stature.

Almond Wreath Celebration Tower

KRANSEKAGE/KRANSEKAKE

GLUTEN-FREE (IF USING CORNMEAL), DAIRY-FREE, VEGETARIAN

MAKES: 1 kransekake, serving a crowd
PREP TIME: 1 hour
COOK TIME: 20 minutes

FOR THE DOUGH

1½ pounds almond flour

1½ pounds confectioners' sugar

½ teaspoon freshly ground cardamom

⅛ teaspoon salt

4 egg whites

1 teaspoon almond extract

Semolina or cornmeal, for dusting the molds

1. To make the dough, in a large mixing bowl, stir the almond flour, confectioners' sugar, cardamom, and salt together. With an electric mixer running, slowly add the egg whites and almond extract, mixing until a dough forms.

2. Transfer the dough to a double boiler and knead the dough for about 10 minutes, working it with your hands until the dough becomes almost too hot to comfortably work with. (For this step I mix the dough in the large mixing bowl I use for my stand mixer, and set this over a saucepan of simmering water.)

3. Preheat the oven to 350°F.

4. Allow the dough to cool a bit, prepping the molds while you wait: Spray them with a baking spray or brush with a neutral oil or softened butter, then dust with semolina or cornmeal.

FOR THE ICING

1 pound confectioners' sugar

3 egg whites

1 tablespoon lemon juice

TIP: If you have extra dough, just roll this into separate cookies and bake, then drizzle with melted, tempered chocolate later. (See the Technique Tip on page 61 for instructions for tempering chocolate.)

SERVING TIP: Serve *kransekake* from the bottom up. By removing rings from the bottom, you preserve the integrity of the rest of the cake and maintain an attractive appearance.

5. Form the dough into logs about the thickness of a finger and arrange them in the molds.

6. Slide these into the oven and bake for about 10 minutes, or until light gold. Allow to cool before assembling (some people even freeze the rings for 24 hours at this point, which some believe enhances the texture).

7. To make the icing, whisk together the confectioners' sugar, egg whites, and lemon juice. Transfer this to a pastry bag fitted with a small tip.

8. To assemble, place the largest ring on your serving plate or cake stand, attaching it with a little of the icing. Pipe the icing over it in a curved zigzag manner, letting it form a decorative scalloped shape on the sides, then set the next largest ring on top. Repeat with the remaining rings, working biggest to smallest, until you reach the top.

This beloved Norwegian classic is nothing short of spectacular. While humble in appearance, the cake's defining flavors of almond and cardamom—classic ingredients in Norwegian baking—make each bite truly memorable. To me, this is the quintessential Norwegian coffee treat. If you enjoy marzipan candy, you'll love this dessert.

Raspberry-Filled Cardamom and Almond Prince Cake

FYRSTEKAKE

VEGETARIAN

MAKES: 1 (9-inch) tart
PREP TIME: 30 minutes, plus time to chill
COOK TIME: 40 minutes

FOR THE CRUST

2¼ cups all-purpose flour

⅔ cup confectioners' sugar

12 tablespoons (1½ sticks) cold butter, cubed

1 egg

FOR THE FILLING

3 cups almond flour

¾ cup sugar

3 eggs

1½ tablespoons butter

¾ teaspoon freshly ground cardamom

1 teaspoon vanilla extract

½ teaspoon almond extract

1 cup raspberry jam

1. To make the crust, in a food processor, whirl the flour, sugar, and butter together until crumbly, then add the egg and process until it comes together into a dough (take care to not overwork). Form the dough into two disks, one with three-fourths of the dough, the other with the remaining fourth. Cover with plastic wrap and refrigerate for at least 2 hours.

2. Preheat the oven to 350°F. Grease a 9-inch tart pan with a removable bottom.

3. On a lightly floured surface, roll out the larger amount of dough until it's a circle large enough to fit the pan. Place it into the bottom of the pan, using your hands to work it into the crease and up the sides. (Alternatively, shape the dough into a rough disk, flatten it a bit, and then form it into the pan using your hands.)

4. To make the filling, in a food processor, whirl the almond flour, sugar, eggs, butter, cardamom, vanilla extract, and almond extract together until combined.

5. Spread the raspberry jam across the bottom of the tart shell, then top with the almond filling, carefully smoothing it with a spatula.

FOR THE TOPPING

1 egg yolk

1 tablespoon water

6. Roll out the remaining disk of dough onto a lightly floured surface so it's roughly ⅛-inch thick. Cut into 1-inch-wide strips and arrange in a lattice or crisscross design on top of the filling.

7. To make the topping, in a small bowl, beat the egg yolk and water together with a fork and brush across the top of the cake.

8. Bake for 40 minutes, or until golden on top. Cool on a wire rack, then remove from the pan.

VARIATION TIP: Make this dairy-free by using vegan butter.

Somehow, I lived most of my nearly four decades without tasting this unique wonder of a cake. My favorite part is the buttery brown sugar topping that infuses the crumb with a caramel-like flavor. And since it's made with yeast, this fluffy Danish cake has a texture akin to coffee cake but somehow even more satisfying.

Yeasted Brown Sugar and Butter Cake
BRUNSVIGER

NUT-FREE, VEGETARIAN

MAKES: 16 servings
PREP TIME: 1 hour 20 minutes, plus time to cool
COOK TIME: 45 minutes

FOR THE DOUGH

8 tablespoons (1 stick) butter

1 cup milk

2 packets (4½ teaspoons) active dry yeast

¼ cup sugar, divided

2 eggs

½ teaspoon ground cardamom

½ teaspoon salt

4 cups all-purpose flour

FOR THE TOPPING

12 tablespoons (1½ sticks) butter

1½ cups packed brown sugar, plus more for decorating

½ teaspoon cinnamon

1. To make the dough, in a small saucepan, melt the butter. Pour in the milk and let it cool to 110°F, then pour a little of the mixture over the yeast and ½ teaspoon sugar. Let this proof until it bubbles, 5 to 10 minutes.

2. Add the eggs, remaining milk and sugar, cardamom, and salt and stir to combine. Stir in the flour, using your hands, if needed, to mix it all in. Let rise, covered, for 30 minutes, or until doubled.

3. Butter or spray a 9-by-13-inch baking pan. Spread the dough in the pan and cover and let it rise another 20 minutes.

4. Preheat the oven to 400°F.

5. To make the topping, in a small saucepan, melt the butter over medium heat along with the brown sugar and cinnamon.

6. Use your finger to poke holes all over the top of the dough, then pour the topping over, spreading it evenly. Sprinkle more brown sugar over this, then bake about 20 minutes, or until the topping is bubbling.

7. Let cool in the pan for about 20 minutes, then cut and serve warm.

Swedish *ostkaka* bears no resemblance to the American cheesecake. Instead of the graham cracker crust and sweetened cream cheese filling, *ostkaka* begins with cottage cheese and is a self-contained cake, no crust required. While modern *ostkaka* recipes often begin with commercial cottage cheese, the original began with milk and rennet. That's how my husband's great-aunt Anna-Lisa did it, and that's what I'm sharing here.

Anna-Lisa's Cheesecake

🇸🇪 OSTKAKA

VEGETARIAN

MAKES: 1 (8-inch) cake
PREP TIME: 2 hours
30 minutes, including time
for the milk and rennet to
set and drain
COOK TIME: 1 hour 15 minutes

2 cups whole milk

¾ cup all-purpose flour

¼ vegetarian rennet tablet

4 eggs

½ cup heavy whipping cream

¼ cup ground almonds

¼ cup sugar

½ teaspoon almond extract

Confectioners' sugar,
   for dusting

Raspberry jam, for serving

Fresh berries, for serving

1. In a small saucepan, heat the milk to 110°F. Stir in the flour and rennet and let it sit for about 1½ hours, or until thick, stirring occasionally at first while the rennet dissolves. Drain in a cheesecloth for 30 minutes, then refrigerate until you're ready to bake (this can be done a day in advance).

2. Preheat the oven to 350°F. Butter an 8-inch springform pan, line the bottom with parchment paper, and spray the paper with nonstick cooking spray.

3. In a mixing bowl, beat the eggs, whipping cream, almonds, sugar, and almond extract to combine. Cut the milk mixture into small pieces and fold it in.

4. Pour the batter into the pan and bake for 1 to 1¼ hours, or until it's golden on top and looks set in the middle.

5. Carefully transfer to a wire rack to cool for several hours, taking care to disrupt it as little as possible.

6. Dust with the confectioners' sugar and serve lukewarm with jam and berries.

TIME-SAVING TIP: While I recommend that you make the recipe as Anna-Lisa did, I realize there will be times when you just don't have the luxury of time. To use store-bought cottage cheese, simply begin with step 3 folding in 1½ cups of commercial full-fat cottage cheese instead of the homemade version.

Cookies

MANY OF MY MEMORIES OF CHRISTMASTIME took place in the kitchens and dining rooms of my mom and my grandmothers. Grandma Adeline would drape clear plastic sheets over the furniture come autumn, in preparation for baking *lefse* (see page 26 for her recipe). Once she and my grandfather had frozen an adequate amount of this potato-based flatbread for the holidays and cleaned away any molecules of errant flour that had crept beyond the plastic sheets, they could relax (a bit, at least) and begin baking cookies. Likewise, now that I've shared with you many of my favorite Scandinavian breads, pastries, and cakes, I'm excited to relax (a bit) and offer you a spread of beloved cookie recipes.

The Scandinavian Christmas season is defined in large part by a very special tradition: *syv slags kaker,* or seven sorts of cookies. According to this custom, all proper Scandinavian households should have seven different kinds of cookies to serve at Christmastime. I only became aware of the tradition as an adult, but there's no doubt that my family's propensity for loading platters with multitudes of cookies stems from that particular part of our heritage.

I never tire of seeing the variety of cookies in the Scandinavian repertoire. With little more than butter, sugar, eggs, and flour—and a scattering of spices—one can create an extensive assortment of treats. Sometimes elegant and elaborate, often simple, the recipes of my heritage have helped me understand more about where my family came from.

In my memories, Grandma Adeline is rarely sitting still; rather, she's on her feet rolling dough or drying dishes, always with an expression of focus and joy on her face. It's with similar joy that I share these recipes with you.

This is the cookie that evokes those blue Danish cookie tins—you know the ones, right? I associate those tins (and these cookies) with Christmas tree shopping and hot apple cider and all the rest of the holiday *hygge* from my childhood. While I usually use vanilla extract or vanilla sugar in my baking, this is one of those recipes in which the bean seems worthwhile—they are vanilla wreaths, after all.

Vanilla-Flecked Butter Wreath Cookies

VANILJEKRANSE

VEGETARIAN

MAKES: About 2 dozen cookies

PREP TIME: 45 minutes, including chilling time

COOK TIME: 16 minutes

8 tablespoons (1 stick) butter, at room temperature

⅓ cup sugar

1 egg

½ vanilla bean, cut in half lengthwise, seeds scraped out

1¼ cups all-purpose flour

¼ cup almond flour

¼ teaspoon salt

1. Preheat the oven to 350°F. Line two baking sheets with parchment paper.

2. In a large mixing bowl, cream the butter and sugar with an electric mixer. Add the egg and vanilla bean seeds, mix well, and then stir in the all-purpose flour, almond flour, and salt until incorporated. Load the dough into a pastry bag fitted with a star tip. Express the dough into wreaths about 2 inches in diameter, arranging them about an inch or so apart on the baking sheets.

3. Slide the pans into the refrigerator to firm up for 15 to 30 minutes so they don't spread, then bake until golden, about 8 minutes. (Bake one sheet at a time in the center of the oven.) Cool on a wire rack, then store in an airtight container. These should last for a few weeks and also freeze well.

TECHNIQUE TIP: Piping the dough demands patience and strength. Do yourself a favor and choose a star-shaped tip that's not too small. You might need to try a few to find one that works best for you.

This recipe is adapted from a couple of handwritten recipes in Grandma Adeline's collection. My mother, Sandi, has been making these for years, and I asked her to share her tips and tricks, which I've woven into the instructions.

Classic Buttery Pressed Cookies

▀▀ SPRITZ

VEGETARIAN

MAKES: About
11 dozen cookies

PREP TIME: 25 minutes, plus
time to chill

COOK TIME: 10 minutes
per sheet

2 cups (4 sticks) butter,
 at room temperature

1 cup granulated sugar

½ cup confectioners' sugar

2 eggs, at room temperature

1 tablespoon vanilla extract

½ teaspoon almond extract

4 cups all-purpose flour

½ teaspoon salt

Sugar sprinkles, for
 topping (optional)

1. Cream the butter, granulated sugar, and confectioners' sugar until the butter is light and smooth. Add the eggs, vanilla extract, and almond extract and mix well. Add the flour and salt and mix until incorporated. Gather the dough up into logs that will fit in your cookie press, then wrap in plastic and chill for about 1 hour before beginning.

2. When you're ready to bake, preheat the oven to 325°F. Load the cookie press with one of the chilled logs and press onto an ungreased baking sheet. Decorate with sprinkles (if using).

3. Bake about 10 minutes, until the cookies are set—they shouldn't quite start to turn color. Rotate the baking sheet as needed.

4. Cool the cookies on a wire rack. Stored in an airtight container, these should last for several weeks.

VARIATION TIP: If you don't have a cookie press, feel free to use a pastry bag with a small star tip to make shapes. Traditionally, these cookies were often shaped as Ss and Os.

TECHNIQUE TIP: Temperature is important to getting these just right. The dough should be chilled but not too cold. The baking sheet should be cool as well. If your first cookies spread while baking, consider chilling the pressed dough on the baking sheet for the remaining cookies before sliding those sheets into the oven to bake.

These tender cookies—presumably named after one of the several Norwegian kings named Håkon—are made with marzipan and coated with pearl sugar, giving them a rich almond flavor and lovely contrast in texture. I'm guessing these will be a favorite on many future holiday cookie platters!

Sugar-Coated Slice-and-Bake Almond Cookies
HÅKONSKAKER/HÅKONKAKOR/HÅKONSKAGER

VEGETARIAN

MAKES: About 4 dozen cookies
PREP TIME: 20 minutes, plus time to chill
COOK TIME: 15 minutes

FOR THE COOKIES

14 tablespoons (1¾ sticks) butter

⅔ cup confectioners' sugar

3½ ounces marzipan

1 teaspoon vanilla extract

¼ teaspoon almond extract

2 cups all-purpose flour

FOR THE COATING

1 egg, beaten

Pearl sugar or other coarse sugar such as demerara

1. For the cookies, mix together the butter, sugar, marzipan, vanilla extract, and almond extract. Add the flour and mix and knead as needed to make a smooth dough without overworking. (It will be a little crumbly, but that's okay.)

2. Shape the dough into logs about 1½ inches in diameter. (The dough will press together easily. Working on a sheet of plastic wrap and using it to roll the dough will help.) Chill for a couple of hours or overnight, or until firm.

3. Preheat the oven to 350°F. Line two baking sheets with parchment paper.

4. Brush the logs with the beaten egg, then roll in the sugar to coat. Cut the logs into ¼-inch slices and place about 1 inch apart on the prepared pans. Bake for 10 to 15 minutes, or until the cookies are set and only begin to show a hint of color.

5. Cool on a wire rack and store in an airtight container.

TECHNIQUE TIP: Since the dough needs to chill before you slice it anyway, consider making dough for these and some other slice-and-bake cookies (such as the almond-studded *bondkakor* on page 104) a day or two in advance. That way, you'll have several logs ready for whenever you have time to bake them in the days that follow.

These sweet little Swedish cookies are almost ethereal, thanks in part to an interesting ingredient: baker's ammonia. Also known as ammonium carbonate and salt of hartshorn, this leavening agent lets off a potent odor when baking (think smelling salts), but while it may surprise you with an offensive odor when you open the oven door, it leaves no trace of this in the finished cookies. I found a recipe for *drömmar* years ago attributed to Alma Halvarson, an old family friend. After both my grandfather Lowell and Alma passed away, Alma's late husband and my grandma Adeline tied the knot, spending some of their later years in each other's good company. So, I like to consider this an adaptation of an old family recipe, in a way.

Vanilla Dream Cookies

🏴 DRÖMMAR

NUT-FREE, EGG-FREE, VEGETARIAN

MAKES: About 2 dozen cookies
PREP TIME: 1 hour, including time to chill
COOK TIME: 20 minutes

8 tablespoons (1 stick) butter, at room temperature

⅔ cup sugar

2 tablespoons neutral vegetable oil

½ teaspoon vanilla extract

1½ cups all-purpose flour

1 teaspoon baker's ammonia

1. In a large mixing bowl, cream the butter and sugar until the mixture is pale and fluffy. Stir in the oil and vanilla to incorporate, then add the flour and baker's ammonia and stir to mix. Press the dough together using your hands, then shape it into balls about the size of small walnuts, about 1 inch in diameter, making them a little taller than they are wide. Arrange them on two ungreased baking sheets about 2 inches apart. Chill for at least 30 minutes.

2. While the cookies chill, preheat the oven to 300°F.

3. Transfer the baking sheets, one at a time, to the oven and bake on the center rack for 15 to 20 minutes, or until the cookies are just barely golden. Let cool on a rack, then store in an airtight container.

VARIATION TIP: See page 6 for more information on where to find baker's ammonia. If you can't find it, try substituting equal parts baking soda and baking powder. The results won't be identical, but these cookies are quite a dream, and I don't want you missing out!

I grew up knowing these cookies—as did many American families, including those with Scandinavian roots—as snowballs. I later heard them called Mexican wedding cookies, and have since heard them described as Russian tea cakes and Danish wedding cookies, plus the very Danish- and Swedish-sounding names of *smør bullar* and *smör bullar*. Even NPR's *The Salt* blog featured an article about them in 2017, calling them Danish but admitting that the origins were somewhat murky. Regardless of where these cookies come from, they're a staple in my family, for sure, as well as many others. This recipe is adapted from the one my family has been using for as long as I can remember.

Pecan-Studded Butter Cookies

SMØR BULLAR/SMÖR BULLAR

EGG-FREE, VEGETARIAN

MAKES: About 2 dozen cookies
PREP TIME: 30 minutes, plus time to chill
COOK TIME: 45 minutes

1 cup (2 sticks) butter, at room temperature

½ cup granulated sugar

2 teaspoons vanilla extract

¼ teaspoon salt

¼ teaspoon baking powder

2 cups all-purpose flour

1 cup finely chopped pecans

Confectioners' sugar, for rolling

1. In a large mixing bowl, cream the butter and sugar with an electric mixer until it's light and fluffy, then stir in the vanilla extract. Add the salt and baking powder, and then the flour a little at a time and beat until it's just incorporated, then stir in the pecans. Chill for at least 30 minutes.

2. While the dough chills, preheat the oven to 275°F. Line two baking sheets with parchment paper.

3. Form the dough into balls about 1 inch in size, and arrange them on the parchment paper about 1 inch apart.

4. Bake for about 45 minutes (depending on the size of the cookies, start checking early), or until they're lightly golden at their base. Transfer the cookies to a wire rack to cool for about 15 minutes, then roll them in confectioners' sugar and let them cool completely before storing in an airtight container.

TECHNIQUE TIP: To coat the cookies with confectioners' sugar, simply roll them in it as directed, or gently shake them, a few at a time, in a bag of confectioners' sugar.

By this point in the book, you've probably noticed my affinity for marzipan and all manners of almond treats. Indeed, almond is a beloved ingredient in Scandinavian baking, and this is one of those recipes in which it is truly the star. These intensely flavored little drops are the essence of almond. Tiny and simple, they are commonly served with *nyponsoppa*, rose hip soup. I've included a recipe for blueberry soup (next page) as an alternative.

Delicate Almond Macaroons

🇩🇰 MANDELBISKVIER

GLUTEN-FREE, DAIRY-FREE, VEGETARIAN

MAKES: About 5 dozen macaroons
PREP TIME: 20 minutes, plus time to chill
COOK TIME: 20 minutes

1 egg white

7 ounces almond paste, grated

½ cup confectioners' sugar

1. In a mixing bowl, beat the egg white with an electric mixer for a moment, then add the almond paste and confectioners' sugar and continue to beat until combined. (Alternatively, you can use a food processor for this step.) Load the dough into a pastry bag fitted with a medium star-shaped tip and pipe it out onto a parchment-paper-lined baking sheet into decorative dollops about ¾ inch in diameter. Slide the baking sheet into the refrigerator to chill for about 1 hour.

2. Preheat the oven to 300°F. Bake for about 20 minutes, or until the macaroons are lightly golden and slightly chewy. Slide the parchment paper onto a wire rack and leave the cookies there to cool.

TECHNIQUE TIP: Take care to not overbake these, as the almond paste will take on a bitter taste.

CHILLED BLUEBERRY SOUP WITH SWEETENED CRÈME FRAÎCHE AND ALMONDS KJØLT BLÅBÆRSSUPPE MED SØTET CRÈME FRAÎCHE OG MANDLER

GLUTEN-FREE, EGG-FREE, VEGETARIAN

MAKES: 4 servings
PREP TIME: 2 hours, including chilling time
COOK TIME: 25 minutes

FOR THE BLUEBERRY SOUP

1 pint (12 ounces) blueberries

1½ cups water, plus
   1 tablespoon, divided

1 tablespoon sugar

¼ teaspoon cinnamon

1 teaspoon potato starch
   (cornstarch will also work)

1 tablespoon lemon juice

1 teaspoon vanilla extract

FOR THE SWEETENED CRÈME FRAÎCHE

¼ cup crème fraîche

½ teaspoon sugar

FOR THE TOPPING

2 tablespoons sliced almonds

1. To make the soup, in a medium pot, bring the blueberries, 1½ cups of water, sugar, and cinnamon to a boil. Reduce the heat and simmer for 5 minutes, stirring every once in a while and using the back of a spoon to crush the berries.

2. Meanwhile, in a small bowl use a fork to mix the potato starch with the remaining tablespoon of water. Add to the soup, increasing the heat to boil for a minute to thicken, stirring constantly. Remove from the heat and stir in the lemon juice and vanilla extract.

3. Cool for about 15 minutes, then transfer to the refrigerator to chill.

4. To serve, divide the soup among four small bowls.

5. In a small bowl, stir the crème fraîche and sugar together. Spoon it over the soup and use a toothpick or tip of a knife to spread it around the surface in an attractive design. Sprinkle with the almonds and serve.

VARIATION TIP: Omit the sweetened crème fraîche to make this recipe dairy-free and vegan. To make it nut-free, simply leave out the almond topping.

TIP: To make your own crème fraîche, simply pour 1 cup of heavy whipping cream and 2 tablespoons of buttermilk in a pint-sized jar. Cover with a square of cheesecloth and fasten it with string or a rubber band. Let sit at room temperature, around 70°F, until thickened, about 24 hours. Stir until it appears smooth, then seal and refrigerate.

There are all sorts of exquisite and delicate cookies in the Scandinavian baking repertoire, and as special as they are (and fun to make!), I most appreciate something that comes together simply yet leaves me returning for bite after bite. These almond-studded slice-and-bake cookies do just that. If you can get your hands on golden syrup, please do—it lends a lovely, complex sweetness to these cookies.

Crispy Farmer Cookies with Golden Syrup and Almonds
BONDKAKOR

VEGETARIAN

MAKES: About 4 dozen cookies
PREP TIME: 20 minutes, plus time to chill
COOK TIME: 12 minutes

14 tablespoons (1¾ sticks) butter, at room temperature

¾ cup sugar

1½ tablespoons golden syrup or molasses

½ teaspoon vanilla extract

¼ teaspoon almond extract

2 cups all-purpose flour

1 cup coarsely chopped almonds

1 teaspoon baking soda

¼ teaspoon salt

1. In a mixing bowl, cream the butter and sugar together. Add the golden syrup or molasses, vanilla extract, and almond extract and stir to combine. Add the flour, almonds, baking soda, and salt and mix to incorporate.

2. Roll the dough into 2 or 3 logs, each 1½ inches in diameter. Chill for at least 1 hour or overnight.

3. Preheat the oven to 350°F. Line two baking sheets with parchment paper. Cut the cookies into ¼-inch slices and place on the baking sheets about 1½ inches apart. Bake for 10 to 12 minutes, or until set, then cool on a wire rack.

4. Store in an airtight container.

If you can imagine a brownie crossed with a double chocolate cookie, you're a step toward wrapping your mind around these incredible cookies. With a touch of rye (which complements the chocolate perfectly) and a dusting of flaky salt, these cookies are sure to make delicious conversation starters at the holiday cookie table.

Salted Chocolate and Rye Cookie Slices
CHOKLAD-RÅGSNITTAR

NUT-FREE, VEGETARIAN

MAKES: About 2 dozen cookie slices
PREP TIME: 20 minutes
COOK TIME: 30 minutes

12 tablespoons (1½ sticks) butter, at room temperature

1 cup sugar

1 egg

1 teaspoon vanilla extract

1¼ cups all-purpose flour

¾ cup rye flour

½ cup cocoa powder

2 teaspoons instant espresso powder

1 teaspoon baking powder

¼ teaspoon salt

¼ cup cacao nibs

1 beaten egg

1 teaspoon flaky salt

2 teaspoons pearl sugar

1. Preheat the oven to 350°F. Line a baking sheet with parchment paper.

2. In a mixing bowl, cream the butter and sugar with an electric mixer until light. Add the egg and vanilla and combine.

3. In a separate bowl, whisk together the all-purpose flour, rye flour, cocoa powder, espresso powder, baking powder, and salt, then pour the flour mixture into the butter mixture and stir to combine. Stir in the cacao nibs.

4. Roll the dough into 2 or 3 logs about 1½ inches in diameter. Place these on the baking sheet and flatten them a little. Brush with the beaten egg, then sprinkle with flaky salt and pearl sugar.

5. Bake for 25 to 30 minutes, or until the cookies are set but still slightly soft when you press lightly in the center. Cool a little, then slice at an angle 1 inch apart.

6. Cool completely on a wire rack, then store in an airtight container.

In the US, we call a variation of these "thumbprint cookies," but in Sweden they're known as *hallongrottor*—raspberry caves—or *rosenmunnar*. They're typically flavored with vanilla and filled with raspberry jam, hence the name, but I couldn't resist adding some almond and cardamom to the mix. For those of you who follow my Scandinavian food blog, *Outside Oslo*, you may recollect a similar recipe incorporating almond, cardamom, and lingonberry jam—one of the most popular recipes on my site—but dog-ear this page anyway, as this is a different recipe and quite worth making.

Raspberry-Filled Almond Cups
HALLONGROTTA

GLUTEN-FREE, EGG-FREE, VEGETARIAN

MAKES: About 2 dozen cookies
PREP TIME: 25 minutes
COOK TIME: 14 minutes

12 tablespoons (1½ sticks) butter

¾ cup sugar

½ teaspoon almond extract

½ teaspoon vanilla extract

1 cup almond flour

1¼ cups gluten-free flour

1 teaspoon baking powder

½ teaspoon freshly ground cardamom

¼ teaspoon salt

Raspberry jam, for filling

Confectioners' sugar, for dusting

1. Preheat the oven to 400°F.

2. In a large bowl, cream the butter and sugar using an electric mixer. Add the almond extract and vanilla extract and combine, then stir in the almond flour and gluten-free flour, baking powder, cardamom, and salt until the dry ingredients are just incorporated.

3. Shape the dough into walnut-size balls and put in regular-size cupcake liners placed on a baking sheet.

4. Press down and make a little nest in the top of each ball and tuck in about ¼ teaspoon of jam.

5. Bake for about 14 minutes, or until light. Let set a few minutes on the pan, then transfer to a wire rack to cool.

6. Spoon a little more raspberry jam into the center of each cookie, then dust with confectioners' sugar.

VARIATION TIP: Almond, raspberry, and chocolate is an almost magical flavor combination, so while a drizzle of chocolate glaze wouldn't be traditional, it certainly wouldn't be out of the question!

NOTE: These do not look like the typical thumbprint cookies: The jam sinks into the batter while baking, which is quite lovely as the berry flavor mingles with the almond.

My paternal grandparents and father emigrated from Norway to the United States in 1956, leaving behind their country and family and home when my grandparents were around the age of 40. Nearing that age myself, it's hard to imagine such a monumental transition. My grandparents preserved many Norwegian traditions throughout the rest of their lives, and Grandma Agny shared them generously through her hospitality and cooking. However, I've only found three of her recipes, one of them being these *bryte havrekake*. Translating roughly to "broken oatmeal cookies," these look rather unremarkable with only four ingredients—butter, oatmeal, egg, and sugar—yet the results are rich and flavorful.

Grandma Agny's Oatmeal Cookies
BRYTE HAVREKAKE

GLUTEN-FREE, NUT-FREE, VEGETARIAN

MAKES: About 2 dozen cookies
PREP TIME: 15 minutes
COOK TIME: 15 minutes

1 cup (2 sticks) butter

3 cups old-fashioned rolled oats

1 cup sugar

1 egg

1. Preheat the oven to 300°F. Line two baking sheets with parchment paper.

2. In a medium saucepan, melt the butter and then add the oats, letting them heat for a couple of minutes, or until they just begins to take on a golden glow, then remove from the heat and let them cool for a few minutes.

3. In a separate bowl, stir the sugar and egg together until the sugar begins to dissolve. Add the oats and stir to combine, then drop from a teaspoon onto the prepared baking sheet.

4. Bake for about 10 minutes, or until the cookies are golden and firm.

Scandinavian Christmas cookies can be baked, cooked on an iron, or fried, as you'll see in the next few recipes. This particular one—rich in butter and made with a dough that incorporates both hard-cooked and raw egg yolks—is a true classic. In 1992, *Aftenposten*, Norway's largest daily paper, conducted a survey of Norwegian Christmas cookies, and *Berlinerkranser* were among the most popular. This particular recipe is very good, if I do say so myself, and while I've shared it before, I couldn't resist including it here. The cookies, especially when warm out of the oven, are rich and eggy, warm and comforting. Be sure to indulge in one or two—perhaps with a cup of coffee—before setting them out for guests.

Buttery Berlin Wreath Cookies

BERLINERKRANSER/ÄGGKRINGLOR

NUT-FREE, VEGETARIAN

MAKES: About 2 dozen cookies
PREP TIME: 30 minutes, plus time to chill
COOK TIME: 10 minutes

2 hard-cooked egg yolks

2 eggs, separated

⅔ cup sugar

2½ cups all-purpose flour

1 cup (2 sticks) butter, at room temperature

¼ cup pearl sugar

1. In a mixing bowl, mash the hard-cooked egg yolks with a fork, then mix in the 2 uncooked yolks until smooth. Vigorously whisk in the sugar, then add the flour and the softened butter, alternating, a little at a time. (Work the dough as little as possible; it will still appear crumbly, but it will come together when you press it.) Divide the dough into two thick logs, cover with plastic wrap, and refrigerate for a couple of hours or overnight.

2. When you're getting ready to bake, preheat the oven to 375°F. Line two baking sheets with parchment paper. Remove the dough from the fridge and let it warm up for about 30 minutes before you start shaping them.

3. Divide each piece of dough into 14 even pieces. Put half of the dough back in the fridge to stay cool while you work on the first half—the dough can be challenging to work with as it gets warm. Roll each piece into a rope about ⅓ inch in diameter and about 4 to 4½ inches long. Form each into a wreath with edges overlapping, and press together. Place the cookies on the baking sheets about 2 inches apart. Chill in the refrigerator for at least 15 minutes to help them keep their shape.

4. In a bowl, lightly beat the egg whites. Dip the tops of the chilled cookies into the beaten egg whites and then into the pearl sugar. Bake in the middle rack of the oven for 8 to 10 minutes, or until the cookies are very lightly golden.

5. Allow the cookies to cool a little on the wire rack still on the pan, then when you're confident that they can hold their shape, slide the sheet of parchment paper onto the rack to let them cool completely.

STORAGE TIP: Store in an airtight container for a few days, or freeze if you're planning to make them well in advance.

Back when Grandma Adeline was alive, Mom and I would sit around the kitchen table under her tutelage as we made these cookies. Mom and I would begin pressing the dough into the little tart tins, and Grandma would finish each one, showing us how to form the thinnest shells possible.

As we shaped cookie after cookie, we'd talk and sip wine, and before long we had a cookie sheet full of filled tins ready to slip into the oven.

Baking *sandbakkelser* is another example of how the cookies are not about the final product for me, but about spending time with these dear women, about togetherness and creating memories. They were an excuse to spend special time with people I love.

Grandma Adeline's Almond-Flavored Tart Shell Cookies

⬛⬛⬛ SANDBAKKELSER/MANDELMUSSLOR

VEGETARIAN

MAKES: About 4 dozen cookies, depending on size of tins

PREP TIME: 1½ hours, plus time to chill

COOK TIME: About 10 minutes per baking sheet

1 cup (2 sticks) unsalted butter, at room temperature

1 cup sugar

1 egg

¼ teaspoon vanilla extract

¼ teaspoon almond extract

3 cups all-purpose flour

⅛ teaspoon salt

1. In a large mixing bowl, cream the butter and sugar until light and fluffy. Add the egg, vanilla extract, and almond extract and stir until combined. Add the flour and salt and mix until the dough comes together. Gather the dough together, flatten into a disk, wrap in plastic, and chill for at least 15 minutes.

2. While the dough chills, preheat the oven to 350°F. Now comes the fun part: shaping the cookies. To start, pinch off a little dough and roll into a ball about ¾ inch in diameter. Place into the center of a *sandbakkel* tin (see Tip, next page) using your thumbs to flatten the dough into the mold. Rotating the tin as you go, work the dough out from the center and up the sides. Using your hand, scrape off the excess dough from the top of the tin and set aside while you form the rest of the cookies.

3. When it's time to bake the cookies, arrange them on a baking sheet (if you're using different shapes of tins, try to keep the like tins together in a batch so they cook evenly) and slide them into the oven, baking one sheet at a time.

4. Watch the cookies closely as they bake, as they shouldn't really color much. When they're just starting to take on a slightly golden hue (about 10 minutes), remove the baking sheet from the oven and slide the tins onto a wire rack to cool.

5. After the cookies have cooled for a while, carefully remove them by inverting the tins onto your work surface and giving a little tap. The cookies should pop right out.

SERVING TIP: While these might look like mini tart shells to the unfamiliar, they are indeed considered cookies. And while some people do fill them—perhaps with sweetened whipped cream and fruit preserves—many enjoy them simply as is. Delicate, crisp, and full of flavor, they need nothing else in order to shine.

TIP: *Sandbakkel* tins are available in Scandinavian supply stores, and you should easily be able to find them online. My favorites are the ones handed down from generation to generation in my family, but if you can't get ahold of well-seasoned vintage ones, any should work just fine.

TECHNIQUE TIP: When pressing the dough into the tins, you'll want it to line the bottom as thinly as possible while still holding up when baked. As you work, take special care at the ridge where the bottom connects to the side. Dough tends to collect here, and it's easy to let this part be too thick.

These are a must to make at Christmastime, especially if you know some little ones who like to get in the kitchen and bake. (Anytime you can roll out dough and cut it into any number of shapes, it's going to be a good day, right?) Make the dough in advance and let it chill in the refrigerator overnight. Then you'll be ready to bake cookies at a moment's notice, anytime you have little hands who want to help with rolling and shaping cookies.

There's a saying—supposedly a Norwegian proverb: Cookies are baked with butter and love. Based on my own experiences baking with my children, I can say without a doubt that this is true.

Cut-Out Gingerbread Cookies
PEPPERKAKER/PEPPARKAKOR

NUT-FREE, EGG-FREE, VEGETARIAN

MAKES: About 4 dozen cookies, depending on the size of cookie cutters
PREP TIME: 1 hour, plus time to chill
COOK TIME: 7 minutes per baking sheet

⅔ cup butter

⅔ cup sugar

½ cup golden syrup or molasses

¼ cup heavy cream

1 tablespoon ground cinnamon

1½ teaspoons freshly ground cardamom

1½ teaspoons ground cloves

1½ teaspoons ground ginger

3 cups all-purpose flour

1 teaspoon baking soda

1. In a medium saucepan, mix the butter, sugar, and golden syrup over medium-low heat until the butter melts and the sugar dissolves. Cool a few minutes, then stir in the cream and the spices.

2. In a large mixing bowl, whisk together the flour and the baking soda. Add the butter mixture and stir until the ingredients are incorporated and a dough comes together. Divide into two pieces and wrap each in plastic wrap and refrigerate overnight.

3. When it's time to bake, preheat the oven to 350°F. Line two baking sheets with parchment paper. On a very lightly floured surface, roll out a little of the dough very thin, about ⅛-inch thick. (Keep the other portions chilled—you want the dough you're working with to always be cold.)

4. Cut the dough into the shapes of your choice and transfer to the baking sheets. Bake one pan at a time for 5 to 7 minutes, or until the edges are barely starting to turn color. Remove from the oven and cool on the baking sheet.

5. Store in an airtight container.

VARIATION TIP: Feel free to adjust the spices to suit your tastes. I analyzed many recipes while developing this one and found that recipes generally include both cinnamon and cloves, and often ginger. They vary most notably in the use of black pepper. People have different opinions on its presence, and I omit it. I do, however, use freshly ground cardamom, which I don't always see. Another thing to note is the syrup. It wouldn't be as authentic to use molasses or honey, although there are recipes that use such alternatives with good results (my mother-in-law uses molasses, and hers are fantastic). If you can get your hands on golden syrup, please do—you'll find that it produces a rich sweetness that accents the spices without being cloying or tasting flat.

I came upon my late grandmother Agny's *krumkaker* recipe by accident some years ago. It was nestled among recipe clippings and cards that my other grandma had given to me when she downsized to a retirement community. I'm thankful that Grandma Agny shared her recipe with Grandma Adeline. Written in Grandma Agny's elegant handwriting on a scrap of blue paper, with a personal note saying "good luck," it's a treasure of mine—one of only three recipes of hers that I have. Had she not been generous enough to share it, it never would have made it into my hands.

Cardamom-Scented Cookie Cones with Cloudberry Cream

KRUMKAKER MED MULTEKREM

NUT-FREE, VEGETARIAN

MAKES: About 4 dozen cookies
PREP TIME: 10 minutes, plus hands-on cooking time
COOK TIME: 30 minutes

10 tablespoons (1¼ sticks) butter

1 teaspoon freshly ground cardamom

3 eggs

¾ cup sugar

1 cup all-purpose flour

Up to ½ cup cold water, or as needed to thin batter to the right consistency

Cloudberry Cream (next page), for filling

1. In a small pan, melt the butter over medium heat. Remove from the heat and stir in the cardamom, then let cool a bit.

2. In a mixing bowl, beat the eggs and sugar together until the mixture is light and fluffy. Mix in the cooled butter, then stir in the flour until the batter is smooth. Mix in cold water, a little at a time as needed, to thin the batter almost to the consistency of thick, heavy cream—it should pour well but still coat the back of a spoon.

3. Heat your *krumkaker* iron and lightly grease it with nonstick cooking spray. To bake the cookies, drop a teaspoon of batter into the center of the iron. Bake until both sides are golden (this takes about a minute on my iron). To remove, slip a metal spatula—some people use the tip of a blunt knife—under the cookie and slide it off, then immediately roll into a cone (see Technique Tip on next page) and set aside to cool.

4. Transfer to an airtight container shortly after they've cooled, or serve immediately. They can also be frozen.

5. If you're planning to fill these with the Cloudberry Cream do so just before serving to keep them as crisp as possible.

CLOUDBERRY CREAM MULTEKREM

GLUTEN-FREE, NUT-FREE, EGG-FREE, VEGETARIAN

MAKES: about 3 cups
PREP TIME: 15 minutes

1 cup heavy cream

½ teaspoon sugar

½ teaspoon vanilla extract (or use ½ teaspoon vaniljesukker and omit the sugar)

¼ teaspoon cinnamon

1 cup cloudberry jam

1. In a mixing bowl, beat the cream, sugar, vanilla, and cinnamon until stiff peaks form, then fold in the cloudberry jam.

2. Refrigerate until you're ready to fill the *krumkaker*. Serve any additional *multekrem* in bowls with any sort of crumbly cookie nestled in and a bit of a fresh herb for garnish. They'd also be lovely with the waffles on page 54.

TIP: *Krumkaker* irons are available at many cookware and Scandinavian shops, as well as online. Pick up a couple of cone rollers, too. There are some beautiful, hand-carved ones out there, which would make lovely gifts.

TECHNIQUE TIP: Be patient and give yourself plenty of grace. Some *krumkaker* won't turn out just right, but that's okay—part of the fun is sampling the imperfect cookies as you work. Some years ago when I was learning to make *krumkaker*, I asked Grandma Adeline how to roll them onto the cones without burning my fingers. "You just have to do it," she said. Not satisfied that making *krumkaker* should have to hurt, I posted a question on my Facebook page, asking readers for tips. Some people use rollers from Norway that have a clip attached, which allows you to slide the *krumkaker* off the iron and roll it in one step. Others use a dishcloth or parchment paper as a shield for the hands while rolling. Another great tip I learned from one reader is to keep a small glass of ice water nearby—that way you can cool your fingers immediately after rolling the *krumkaker*. I use one hand to hold the cone at the right angle to the counter and hold a fork in the other hand to guide the cookie around the cone. Give it time and you'll find a method that works for you.

SERVING TIP: While I grew up eating *krumkaker* plain, as many people do, they're also often served with fillings such as whipped cream and berries. The cloudberry cream I've included is very typical. If you can't get ahold of cloudberry preserves, substitute another type, adjusting the sugar as needed.

Gathering the dough into a ball, I inhaled the scent of the cardamom and butter, warm in my hands. Like all those memories from my childhood, the feelings stirring in my heart filled me with a sense of love, a security in belonging. These cardamom-scented treats somehow bring back all those memories of childhood simply with their aroma. To many, *fattigmann*—which can be translated as "poor men"—are an essential part of Christmas, a requisite member of the *syv slags kaker*, or seven sorts of Norwegian Christmas cookies. Cookies of this type are known in other Nordic countries as *klenäter*, *klejner*, *kleina*, and *kleynur*.

Cardamom-Scented Fried "Poor Men"

🇳🇴 🇸🇪 🇩🇰 **FATTIGMANN/KLENÄTER/KLEJNER**

NUT-FREE, VEGETARIAN

MAKES: About 3 dozen cookies

PREP TIME: 30 minutes, plus time to chill

COOK TIME: About 7 minutes per batch

5 egg yolks

⅓ cup sugar

⅓ cup whipping cream

1 to 2 tablespoons Cognac or other brandy

1¾ cups all-purpose flour

1 teaspoon baking powder

½ to 1 teaspoon freshly ground cardamom

¼ teaspoon salt

4 tablespoons (½ stick) butter, melted

Canola oil, for frying

Confectioners' sugar, for dusting

1. In a large mixing bowl, beat the egg yolks and sugar thoroughly. In a separate bowl, whip the cream until stiff peaks form. Gently fold in the cream and brandy. In a small bowl, whisk together the flour, baking powder, cardamom, and salt. Add the dry ingredients a bit at a time to the egg mixture, alternating with the melted butter, adding a little more flour if needed to make a dough that will roll well, but work the dough just as little as needed. Refrigerate overnight.

2. When you're ready to make the *fattigmann*, roll out the dough on a lightly floured surface to about ⅛-inch thick. Cut using a *fattigmann* roller and separate the diamonds. For each cookie, work one of the ends through the slit. I find that it's helpful to hold one end up and give it a slight shake to let gravity gently elongate the dough before placing it in the hot oil.

3. In a heavy pot, heat about 2 inches of oil to 350° to 375°F. Working in batches so they fit in a single layer, fry the *fattigmann*, flipping them with tongs when one side is golden, and removing as soon as the other side colors. Transfer to a paper towel–lined surface to drain and cool slightly, then dust with confectioners' sugar. These are best the day they're made.

TECHNIQUE TIP: As with many other Norwegian Christmas cookies, you'll want to plan ahead for these. Mix up the dough on one day, fry the cookies the next. Ideally you'll use a *fattigman* roller (available at Scandinavian supply stores and online), although you can use a pastry wheel as well.

Grandma Agny's *bryte havrekake* (page 107) and these *havreflarn* are like fraternal twins: alike but different, and each equally special. Like any good parent, if I had to pick my favorite—well, just don't ask me to do it.

Lacy Oat Cookies

■■ ■■ **HAVREFLARN/KNIPLINGSKAGER**

GLUTEN-FREE, VEGETARIAN

MAKES: About 1½ dozen cookies
PREP TIME: 15 minutes
COOK TIME: 20 minutes

8 tablespoons (1 stick) butter

1½ cups old-fashioned rolled oats

1 egg

¾ cup sugar

½ teaspoon vanilla extract

¼ teaspoon almond extract

1 tablespoon gluten-free flour

1 teaspoon baking powder

⅛ teaspoon salt

1. Preheat the oven to 350°F. Line three baking sheets with parchment paper.

2. In a medium saucepan, melt the butter, then remove from the heat and stir in the oats.

3. In a mixing bowl, vigorously beat the egg and sugar until the sugar begins to dissolve, then stir in the buttery oats, vanilla extract, and almond extract. Add the flour, baking powder, and salt and stir to combine.

4. Drop tablespoons of the batter onto the baking sheets about 3 inches apart, to give them space to spread. Bake for about 16 minutes, or until they're golden but not caramelized (it's okay to bake multiple sheets at a time, just check on them midway and swap their positions as needed). Store in an airtight container.

VARIATION TIP: These delicate cookies really need no adornment, but feel free to dip them in melted chocolate for an extra-special treat.

While the grownups enjoy their rum truffles (page 120), the kids can have fun making these. Rolling them in different coatings—confectioners' sugar for the rum truffles and either cocoa powder, coconut, sprinkles, or pearl sugar for these—will help keep the spiked and kid-friendly ones from getting mixed up.

No-Bake Chocolate Oat Balls

CHOKLADBOLLAR/HAVREGRYNSKUGLER

GLUTEN-FREE, NUT-FREE, EGG-FREE, VEGETARIAN

MAKES: About 2 dozen oat balls

PREP TIME: 30 minutes, plus time to chill

1½ cups old-fashioned rolled oats

⅔ cup confectioners' sugar

¼ cup cocoa powder

⅛ teaspoon salt

⅓ cup butter, at room temperature

¼ cup strawberry jelly

Cocoa powder, shredded coconut, sprinkles, or pearl sugar, for coating

1. In a mixing bowl, stir together the oats, confectioners' sugar, cocoa powder, and salt. Add the butter and strawberry jelly and mix to combine.

2. Chill for at least 30 minutes, then form into ¾-inch balls and roll in your choice of coating.

3. Store in the refrigerator and keep chilled until ready to serve.

While the women have historically been the bakers in the family, my father is the king of rum balls and bourbon balls. These truffle-like confections pack quite a punch (he makes them strong), and it's always a treat to get a tin of his confectioners' sugar–coated specialty to keep in the fridge for whenever the mood strikes. This is a riff on his recipe.

Dad's Chocolate-Rum Truffles

▊▊ ROMKUGLER

VEGETARIAN

MAKES: About 2 dozen truffles
PREP TIME: 30 minutes, plus time to chill

1 packed cup (4 ounces) crumbled vanilla wafers or sugar cookies

1 cup (4 ounces) finely chopped pecans

1 cup confectioners' sugar, plus more for coating

¼ cup cocoa powder

1 teaspoon instant espresso powder

6 tablespoons rum

1½ tablespoons maple syrup

1. In a medium bowl, mix together the cookie crumbs, pecans, confectioners' sugar, cocoa powder, and espresso powder. Pour in the rum and maple syrup and stir until thoroughly incorporated.

2. Chill for at least 30 minutes, then form the mixture into ¾-inch balls and roll in confectioners' sugar.

3. Store in the refrigerator and keep chilled until ready to serve. These should last for several weeks.

VARIATION TIP: To make these gluten-free, simply choose a variety of dense gluten-free butter or sugar cookies and a brand of confectioners' sugar that's made without gluten.

TECHNIQUE TIP: While I use a food processor to crumble the cookies and chop the nuts, I wouldn't recommend using it to mix the dough entirely—you want the cookies and nuts to retain a hint of their texture.

Measurement Conversions

VOLUME EQUIVALENTS (LIQUID)

US STANDARD	US STANDARD (OUNCES)	METRIC (APPROXIMATE)
2 TABLESPOONS	1 FL. OZ.	30 ML
¼ CUP	2 FL. OZ.	60 ML
½ CUP	4 FL. OZ.	120 ML
1 CUP	8 FL. OZ.	240 ML
1½ CUPS	12 FL. OZ.	355 ML
2 CUPS OR 1 PINT	16 FL. OZ.	475 ML
4 CUPS OR 1 QUART	32 FL. OZ.	1 L
1 GALLON	128 FL. OZ.	4 L

OVEN TEMPERATURES

FAHRENHEIT (F)	CELSIUS (C) (APPROXIMATE)
250°	120°
300°	150°
325°	165°
350°	180°
375°	190°
400°	200°
425°	220°
450°	230°

VOLUME EQUIVALENTS (DRY)

US STANDARD	METRIC (APPROXIMATE)
⅛ TEASPOON	0.5 ML
¼ TEASPOON	1 ML
½ TEASPOON	2 ML
¾ TEASPOON	4 ML
1 TEASPOON	5 ML
1 TABLESPOON	15 ML
¼ CUP	59 ML
⅓ CUP	79 ML
½ CUP	118 ML
⅔ CUP	156 ML
¾ CUP	177 ML
1 CUP	235 ML
2 CUPS OR 1 PINT	475 ML
3 CUPS	700 ML
4 CUPS OR 1 QUART	1 L

WEIGHT EQUIVALENTS

US STANDARD	METRIC (APPROXIMATE)
½ OUNCE	15 G
1 OUNCE	30 G
2 OUNCES	60 G
4 OUNCES	115 G
8 OUNCES	225 G
12 OUNCES	340 G
16 OUNCES OR 1 POUND	455 G

Resources

References

WHERE TO FIND SCANDINAVIAN BAKING SUPPLIES:

Scandinavian Specialties (Seattle, WA and online)

www.scanspecialties.com

Ingebretsen's (Minneapolis, MN; Stockholm, WI; and online)

www.ingebretsens.com

King Arthur Flour (online; for Pullman loaf pan, rye chops, and other baking supplies)

shop.kingarthurflour.com

CHAPTER ONE: BAKING LIKE A SCANDINAVIAN

Stoker—www.edibleseattle.com /recipe/desserts-recipe/norwegian -christmas-cookies

Danish monarchy among the oldest in the world—www.visitdenmark.com /denmark/things-do/history-and-culture /danish-royal-family

Denmark, one of the most prosperous countries—www.en.wikipedia.org/wiki /Economy_of_Denmark

www.eh.net/encyclopedia/an-economic -history-of-denmark

Barley oldest grain—www.sciencedaily .com/releases/2019/04/190403113931.htm

CHAPTER THREE: COFFEE BREADS AND PASTRIES

www.seriouseats.com/2011/03 /spice-hunting-cardamom-curries-sweets -queen-of-spices.html

Winter Holiday Recipes

BREADS, BUNS, AND FLATBREADS

Rye and Syrup Bread with Fennel, Anise, Caraway, and Orange (*Sirupslimpa*)

Grandma Adeline's Potato Lefse (*Potetlefse*)

Saffron-Scented St. Lucia Buns (*Lussekatter/ Lussebulle*)

Christmas Bread with Raisins and Candied Fruit (*Julekake*)

BEVERAGE

Cozy Spiced and Spiked Mulled Red Wine (*Gløgg/Glögg*)

BREAKFAST

Doughnutty Pancake Puffs (*Æbleskiver/Munker*)

SWEETS

Almond Wreath Celebration Tower (*Kransekage/ Kransekake*)

Vanilla-Flecked Butter Wreath Cookies (*Vaniljekranse*)

Classic Buttery Pressed Cookies (*Spritz*)

Sugar-Coated Slice-and-Bake Almond Cookies (*Håkonskaker Håkonkakor/ Håkonskager*)

Vanilla Dream Cookies (*Drömmar*)

Pecan-Studded Butter Cookies (*Smør Bullar/ Smör Bullar*)

Raspberry-Filled Almond Cups (*Hallongrotta*)

Lacy Oat Cookies (*Havreflarn/ Kniplingskager*)

Buttery Berlin Wreath Cookies (*Berlinerkranser/ Äggkringlor*)

Cut-Out Gingerbread Cookies (*Pepperkaker/ Pepparkakor*)

Cardamom-Scented Cookie Cones with Cloudberry Cream (*Krumkaker med Multekrem*)

Grandma Adeline's Almond-Flavored Tart Shell Cookies (*Sandbakkelser/ Mandelmusslor*)

Cardamom-Scented Fried "Poor Men" (*Fattigmann/ Klenäter/Klejner*)

Dad's Chocolate-Rum Truffles (*Romkugler*)

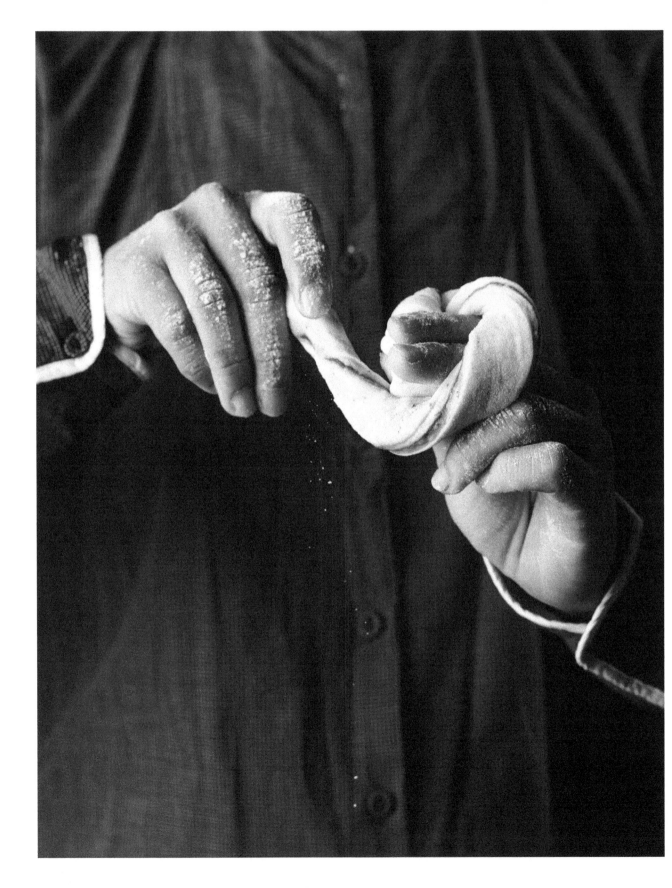

Index

Acknowledgments

AS AN ADULT, I can finally see what a gift all those holidays meals were while I was growing up. Each time my parents or grandparents spread a feast on their dining room table, it was an expression of unconditional love and of selfless hospitality, of our Norwegian American heritage, and of family itself. A gift of belonging, of love, hospitality, generosity, and joy. This book wouldn't exist without all of that. It also wouldn't exist without each of you who have played a role in its creation, from extending your own Scandinavian-laced hospitality or by encouraging me as I've followed my writing dreams.

Elliot, Vincent, and Audrey, you are the heart and the "why" behind my life as a wife and mother. I love you each dearly. V&A, you are the best baking partners and taste-testers, and I appreciate that I can trust you for your honest feedback and kindhearted but constructive criticism. To my parents—Roar and Sandi—it goes without saying that your love and encouragement and support means the world to me.

I also want to recognize my grandparents—Lowell and Adeline, Lauritz and Agny—whose memories I will always cherish, and whose love I carry with me.

I'm throwing out a big hug to my best friend and writing partner, Sarah Madson. Next up, I can't wait to read *your* published book!

To my editor, Rebecca Markley: Thank you for your enthusiasm throughout the process and for making the experience of my debut book such a joy. I wish I could have shared the results of all my recipe testing with you and all the others who worked on the book production—the photographer, designers, publisher, etc.!

Thank you to my literary agent, Deborah Ritchken of Marsal Lyon Literary Agency, for your guidance and wisdom. And thanks to all the influential people who have supported me and provided guidance and encouragement in the book publishing process, including Kathleen Flinn and Ashley Rodriguez.

I'm grateful to my husband's family, for extending the joy of your Swedish heritage.

And finally, a big shoutout to my amazing recipe testers—Sandi Danielsen, Meagan Davenport, Julie Hubert, Jacqueline Jensen, Jamie Midstokke, Jenifer Smith, and Gabrielle Weik.

About the Author

I'VE ALWAYS BEEN A WRITER, but there's part of me that belongs in the kitchen as much as at the desk. Trained as a journalist in college, I began my career as a writer and producer for a morning television newscast in Seattle. Churning out story after story about house fires and wacky weather until the sun rose high, I'd go home in the morning and unwind in the kitchen, leisurely mixing up homemade treats to occasionally bring to the newsroom for the next day's editorial meeting. Until the news director—my mentor—advised me to stop.

"You're going to be known as the newsroom Martha Stewart," he warned me one day. "That's no way for a young, blonde, and attractive woman with an unusual name to gain credibility as a serious journalist," he said. And of course, young and ambitious, I listened.

Now I look back at that time and see how it all makes sense. I had no idea back then, as an aspiring reporter and anchorwoman, that I'd find a way to combine my passions. I've since traded breaking news for food writing and am recognized as a source on Scandinavian cooking. Formerly the food editor for *The Norwegian American*, my work has also appeared in a number of regional and national publications including *Costco Connection*, *The Oregonian*, and *Edible Seattle*, as well as my Scandinavian food blog, called *Outside Oslo*. In 2017 I coedited *A Taste of Norway: Flavors from The Norwegian American*, and I also teach occasional cooking classes in Seattle, where I live. You can find many more Scandinavian recipes on my food blog, *Outside Oslo* (www.outside-oslo.com). Also be sure to stay up-to-date on additional projects including more books, which are in the works, by following along on Instagram (@daytonastrong) and Facebook (www.facebook.com/OutsideOslo/).

Printed in the USA
CPSIA information can be obtained
at www.ICGtesting.com
CBHW042049010524
7764CB00007B/117

9 781646 116188